KINGFISHER KNOWLEDGE

ARCHAEOLOGY

ARCHAEOLOGY

Trevor Barnes

Foreword by
Tony Robinson

KINGFISHER
BOSTON

Editor: Catherine Brereton
Coordinating editor: Caitlin Doyle
Senior designer: Peter Clayman
Cover designer: Anthony Cutting
Picture research manager: Cee Weston-Baker
Consultant: Dr. Miles Russell, Bournemouth University, England
Senior production controller: Debbie Otter
DTP coordinator: Sarah Pfitzner
DTP operator: Primrose Burton
Artwork archivists: Wendy Allison, Jenny Lord
Proofreaders: Sheila Clewley, Jenny Siklos
Indexer: Sue Lightfoot

KINGFISHER
a Houghton Mifflin Company imprint
222 Berkeley Street
Boston, Massachusetts 02116
www.houghtonmifflinbooks.com

First published in hardcover in 2004
First published in paperback in 2007
10 9 8 7 6 5 4 3 2 1
1TR/0807/TWP/MA(MA)130ENSOMA/F

LIBRARY OF CONGRESS CATALOGING-IN-PUBLICATION DATA
Barnes, Trevor.
    Archaeology / Trevor Barnes.—1st ed.
    p. cm.—(Kingfisher knowledge)
    Includes index.
        Summary: Explores the science of excavating and examining debris of
        centuries of human life, from the Iron Age to recent history.
            1. Archaeology—Juvenile literature. [1. Archaeology.] I. Title. II.
        Series.

                C171.B36 2004
                    930.1—dc22
                    2003061916

                ISBN 978-0-7534-6158-7

            Printed in Singapore

NOTE TO READERS
The Web site addresses listed in this book are correct at the time of going
to print. However, due to the ever-changing nature of the Internet, Web site
addresses and content can change. Web sites can contain links that are
unsuitable for children. The publisher cannot be held responsible for changes
in Web site addresses or content or for information obtained through third-party
Web sites. We strongly advise that Internet searches are supervised by an adult.

GO FURTHER . . .
INFORMATION PANEL KEY:

 Web sites and
further reading

 career paths

 places to visit

Contents

Foreword

The trouble with archaeology is that it's so difficult to spell. A lot of people think that a word that has "aeo" in the middle of it must refer to something so complicated that only huge-brained people could possibly understand it. But anyone who thinks this is completely wrong. Archaeology is basically pretty simple. It's the way we can hurtle back into history to discover how people lived hundreds, even thousands, of years ago. And how do we do that? By using detective work. Archaeologists are like the police at a crime scene. They slowly and carefully piece together all of the little bits of evidence that they find on a site in order to work out what was going on there in the dim and distant past.

It may sound like quite a glamorous job, but this evidence is seldom valuable or beautiful to look at. It's garbage. It's the old junk that people have lost, thrown away, or buried throughout history. Don't be fooled by Lara Croft or Indiana Jones. Archaeologists aren't treasure hunters who smash up ancient temples or blow up pyramids in order to snatch some jewel-encrusted casket. Most archaeology is about sifting through broken bits of old pots, handfuls of charred seeds, or pieces of crumbling wood in order to work out what the lives of ordinary people were like in days gone by.

Even the tiniest speck of dust can be important. Eighty years ago, when the English archaeologist Howard Carter discovered the tomb of the Egyptian pharaoh Tutankhamen, he swept it clean before inviting the press in to photograph his fabulous finds. Nowadays archaeologists would give their eyeteeth to get their hands on that dust. All of those tiny dead insects, the strands of hair, and the little fragments of material that ended up in the dustpan would tell us far more about ancient Egypt than a hundred gold chariots.

In Carter's time archaeology was all about digging. But today three weeks on an archaeological site generates three months of activity in the laboratory. There are specialists who can date a piece of wood from the shape of the tree rings, others who can tell whether a site was once wooded, boggy, or covered in trees by examining the shells of long-dead snails. There are people who can work out exactly where a piece of pottery originally came from by looking at the tiny flecks of stone in it, and others who can find out the sex and age of a skeleton and what diseases its owner suffered from.

Digging is still a major part of archaeology. In the 21st century, however, we're much more careful about where we dig. Archaeology is part of our environment. I don't expect you'd dream of chopping down a valued tree or stealing birds' eggs, because you know you'd be damaging something precious. But some people still damage burial sites or dig coins out of archaeological sites and keep them. Most of them don't realize that they're destroying something irreplaceable. Archaeologists do. They only dig part of a site and leave the rest for future generations. They record what they find and where they found it and make sure everything is properly labeled and sent to a museum.

Archaeologists are time travelers, detectives, and friends of the environment. Sounds good, doesn't it? Dive into this book and join them in exploring some of the most amazing archaeological sites in the world.

Tony Robinson—president, Young Archaeologists' Club and presenter of British TV show *Time Team*

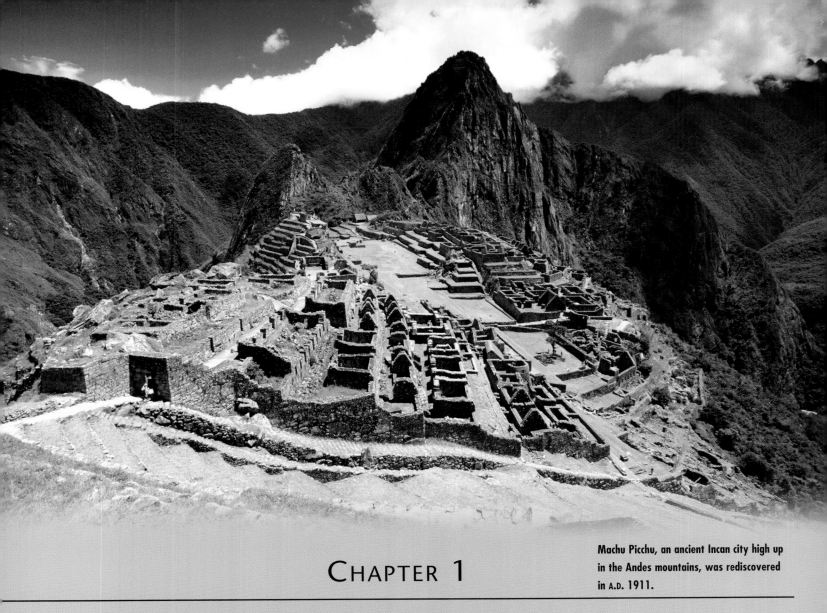

Machu Picchu, an ancient Incan city high up in the Andes mountains, was rediscovered in A.D. 1911.

What is archaeology?

Archaeology is partially about things but mostly about people. The excitement of archaeology lies in building up a picture of human life hundreds, even thousands, of years ago, by making connections between things found in the ground and the people who left them there long ago. Often the physical objects left behind are simple things—tools, toys, weapons, household goods, and coins. They could be fragments of buildings—a piece of a wall, barn, or road—or great structures such as Egyptian temples, Greek amphitheaters, or even entire cities like the ancient Incan capital of Machu Picchu. But what they all have in common is that they have survived, while the people who made and lived with them have been dead a long time. If these remains could speak, what exciting tales they would tell? Archaeology tries to be their voice.

Introducing archaeology

▲ General Augustus Pitt-Rivers (1827–1900) excavated prehistoric sites in southern England. He helped pave the way for modern techniques.

Archaeology is the hands-on study of the past. It involves the excavation or examination of sites and the careful study and analysis of material remains left by people who once lived or worked there. Many of the finds that are unearthed go on public display, but archaeology is not only about collecting objects. For archaeologists it is about understanding. Finding a treasure in a 5,000-year-old pyramid is exciting. Even more exciting is understanding why people put such a treasure there in the first place.

When did it begin?

People have always been interested in the past and in revered objects and places that were important to their ancestors. We know that King Nebuchadrezzar II of Babylon (see pages 32–33) excavated parts of his city more than 2,500 years ago. Babylonian princesses kept the antique objects that were found in their own private rooms. In the 1500s and 1600s there was a fashion of "cabinets of curiosities" in which rich people could display interesting or valuable objects. But archaeology as the systematic process of understanding the past, as we know it, did not begin until the late 1700s.

The start of modern archaeology

In 1784 the man who was to become the third President of the United States, Thomas Jefferson (1743–1826), pioneered a new approach to excavation. While examining Native American burial mounds on his land, he decided that simply digging deeper and deeper to see what objects could be found was imprecise. So he cut a large slice out of one mound and analyzed the various levels, or strata, of material. He carried out a scientific examination of the soil and the skeletons. Scientific thought became as important as the digging itself.

▼ This imaginary scene shows archaeologists excavating the ruins of an ancient classical temple. Like the fictional archaeologist and adventurer Indiana Jones, they are unearthing amazing treasures. But archaeology is just as much about examining garbage and debris, and the less extraordinary sites are just as important as the spectacular ones in building a picture of life in the past.

▲ American statesman, philosopher, and president Thomas Jefferson is often referred to as the father of modern archaeology. He was one of the first people to take a systematic, scientific approach to excavation.

Archaeology and adventure

In the 1800s and early 1900s major excavations were taking place in the Middle East, and archaeology could seem like an adventure. Men like Heinrich Schliemann (see page 16) used their personal wealth to finance expeditions. On the other side of the world the American diplomat John Lloyd Stephens (1805–1852) led explorations deep into the Mexican jungle, where he discovered the ruined cities of the ancient Mayan people, who had lived there centuries earlier.

◄ Archaeology takes objects, such as this amulet discovered in the grave of a 6th-century B.C. Celtic chief in Hochdorf, Germany, and asks where they fit into a picture of the past. Burying such a beautiful, well-crafted object suggests that this society placed great importance on funeral rituals.

A scientific discipline

Archaeology is definitely exciting, but it is not really about adventures and treasures. It is a scientific discipline that uses the objects unearthed at dig sites—including everyday items and garbage, as well as magnificent treasures—as the basis for study. Once archaeologists have collected their objects, they get to work in laboratories, examining the remains and making sense of all of the evidence. Even Indiana Jones (based on the real-life American archaeologist Hiram Bingam, 1875–1956) is portrayed as a scholar and college professor.

What do archaeologists do?

Many people study the past. Archaeologists like to get their hands on it! Of course they read written accounts of earlier civilizations, but they mostly rely on the physical objects that have been left behind by people in the past. Archaeologists explore a site, sifting through evidence and making a detailed examination of clues. Even the tiniest pieces of evidence can help them build a picture of life long ago.

◄ Some of the things that archaeologists study are spectacular. Here they are measuring moai, the vast stone statues on Easter Island in the Pacific Ocean. These remarkable statues were built between 1600 and 100 B.C.

Examining a site

Once archaeologists have identified an area that they believe contains evidence of the past, they start a detailed examination, or dig. Usually they dig a narrow section called a trench. Larger sites are divided up so that a team can carry out a systematic examination. Archaeologists make careful notes of where objects have been discovered and mark them on plans and drawings. They take great care not to damage fragile objects or lose track of exactly where things are found—an object's position is just as important as what it actually is. They use simple tools, such as trowels and brushes, in order to remove soil or sand. Sometimes more sophisticated machinery is needed such as radar or echolocation equipment. By sending electrical charges into the ground, these detect objects hidden beneath the dirt.

Layers of time

One of the main questions archaeologists need to answer is: how old is the evidence they are digging up? The dig site itself can help. On sites where there has been constant human activity the ground level rises over the years as people build on top of what previous generations have left behind. Material builds up in layers called strata. Each layer dates from a different period in history, and studying them helps archaeologists figure out the relative ages of the objects that they find. Other techniques are also useful. Carbon dating measures radioactivity in order to tell the age of organic objects such as bone and plant material. Scientists can also tell the age of a wooden object from tree ring patterns.

▲ These decayed timbers may not look very exciting at first glance, but an archaeologist examining them can uncover a lot of information. They belong to a merchant ship dating back to A.D. 1465. It sank when it had just returned from Portugal with a cargo of cork bark, and it is the only surviving vessel of its type. It was discovered during an excavation project for a new riverside building in Newport, Wales, in 2002.

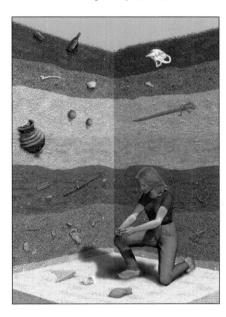

▶ This diagram shows layers of material, or strata, in an imaginary trench in Great Britain. In the top layer are modern items of garbage such as a bottle, can, and plastic bag. Farther down are crockery and clay pipes from the 1700s, a cannon and a sword from the 1600s, and a medieval pot. Then there are a comb and spearhead from Viking times (late A.D. 700s) and a gold buckle and other jewelry from the Anglo-Saxon period (c. A.D. 440–1066). At the base of the trench the archaeologist has found a Roman helmet and beaker (c. A.D. 100). No real trench would be so clearly layered or contain so many treasures though!

History and prehistory

Archaeologists study such a vast span of time—from more than 10,000 years ago until the present day—that they need to divide it into periods. "History" is the time for which we have written records as well as physical remains—from around 3000 B.C. in Mesopotamia but later elsewhere in the world. "Prehistory" is the time before this, and it is divided up into the Stone Age, Bronze Age, and Iron Age—named after the main materials used during these periods. Before 8000 B.C. people made tools out of stone. Around 4000 B.C. they began to develop bronze items, and even later (c. 1400 B.C.) they started to use iron. It is impossible to date these periods accurately because they vary throughout the world and even overlap.

Where is archaeology?

▲ This remarkably well-preserved corpse of an Iron Age man, over 2,000 years old, was found by chance in a peat bog in Jutland, Denmark, in 1950. A noose around his neck indicates that he died by hanging. His stomach still contained his last meal—wild grains and grasses.

Evidence of the past is everywhere. Sometimes it is right under our noses—a Pueblo town in the southwestern U.S., a Saxon church at the end of an English lane, or the ruins of a Crusader castle on a Middle Eastern hilltop. But sometimes the evidence is hidden from view, and archaeologists need to search for less obvious clues.

Physical remains

Ancient ruins provide us with the most visible clues about the past. The physical remains of buildings, whether in brick, stone, or timber, tell us that people once lived or worked there. The archaeologist's task is to explore even more thoroughly. Slowly excavating the site, teams will carefully search for artifacts before recording and storing them for later analysis.

Clues from the land

Sometimes what remains of an earlier construction is not immediately obvious. Stones might have been removed to make other buildings somewhere else, or timbers may have rotted away. Even if nothing is visible at ground level, a view from a different angle can tell a different story. Strange marks on the ground—bushes growing in perfect circles or in completely straight lines following the contours of man-made ditches, for example—show that human hands have been at work. Archaeologists use technology, such as aerial photography, echolocation equipment, geophysical surveys, and satellite photography, to find out more about what is buried beneath the surface.

◀ Sometimes ancient pictures will spark off a search for the historical site where they occurred. This is Sargon, king of the ancient city of Kish in Mesopotamia (now Iraq), around 2350 B.C. He founded another city, Akkad, nearby. This city has yet to be discovered.

▼ Details that could easily be missed at ground level become clear when viewed from the air. An aerial view of Navan fort in Northern Ireland shows that this fortress (dating from 700 B.C.) has a protective ditch and is surrounded by a defensive bank.

Written evidence

Records, such as maps and historical documents, also tell us that particular sites have been associated with human activity over the years. A map produced in the 1700s, for example, may show a building that is no longer standing. But excavation may reveal that its foundations still remain below the surface of the soil—and tell us whether it has been used for different purposes over the centuries.

Chance finds

The most exciting discoveries are often made by chance. In 1940 boys walking in the woods in Lascaux in southwestern France found prehistoric cave paintings that had been hidden for 15,000 years (see pages 20–21). Sometimes freak weather conditions give luck a helping hand. In 1991 a partial thaw of a glacier in northern Italy revealed the body of a Bronze Age man, perfectly preserved by the ice for more than 5,000 years.

▲ This map of Tenochtitlán (see pages 50–51) exaggerates the size of the sacred enclosure at the heart of the city, which amazed the Spanish who made the map in the 1500s. Maps such as this are full of clues for archaeologists.

Bits and pieces

No object is too big or too small for an archaeologist to study. Whether it is a whole city that has laid undisturbed in the mountains for centuries or a Roman coin no bigger than a thumbnail, each object that comes to light is a vital clue to the past. An archaeologist is a type of historical detective who pieces together clues to try to build a complete picture. But every time a new piece of evidence emerges, the picture changes. Questions could be answered, or new mysteries could emerge. Far from staying still, our understanding of the past is constantly evolving.

Three-dimensional jigsaw puzzles

Archaeologists love jigsaw puzzles—in three dimensions and without pictures to guide them. They might find a small piece of pottery as they excavate a site. Then they find another, and another, and before long they are piecing together fragments of a jar that was used 2,000 years ago. Careful analysis of the inside of the jar will show what it was used for—storing grain, water, wine, or olive oil. Some pottery fragments are very elaborate. For example, vases from Athens in the 500s B.C. show scenes from everyday Athenian life and tell us a lot about society in ancient Greece.

▲ This silver coin was minted during the time of Ptolemy I, who reigned over Egypt from 304 B.C. Coins are easy to date because the ruler shown will have been historically documented. They may be found thousands of miles from their origin, shedding light on patterns of trade.

▲ An archaeologist examines everyday garbage from long ago—an oyster shell mound unearthed along the banks of the river at the site of St. Mary's City, believed to be the earliest settlement in modern-day Maryland. Shellfish, such as oysters, were an important food source in early riverside settlements.

▶ Pictures from the past show us how people worked or played and what they looked like. Sometimes a single vivid picture can speak louder than words, giving us a sense of connection with an ancient civilization. This wall painting from the Palace of Knossos (see pages 34–35) shows two boys boxing.

▶ It's not just the important buildings and precious objects that can survive for centuries. Unusual circumstances, such as burial by volcanic ash, can mean remarkable finds—like this bowl of olives found in Pompeii (see pages 42–43), preserved for almost 2,000 years.

Human remains

Sometimes the fragments archaeologists study are human remains. Skulls, bones, and teeth can tell us a lot about the injuries people suffered, the types of foods they ate, and how they died. Burial mounds, graves, and tombs are full of this type of detail. The way in which the dead were buried can help us build up a picture of how the living organized their societies. Graves often contain artifacts, such as jewelry and weapons, and give us an indication of what the people buried there thought about death. Many believed that death was the start of a new life somewhere else—so they buried the dead with objects that they thought would help on the journey through the afterlife.

Garbage

While treasures and riches are exciting and important, much of what archaeologists find is garbage—objects lost, broken, or thrown away as part of everyday life. This garbage often tells us the most about a site and the people who lived there. What might future generations think about the bits and pieces you throw away?

▼ Ornamental objects can tell us about a society's beliefs and customs. This head depicting a coyote warrior—an important figure—is from the Toltec civilization, who lived in South America more than 3,000 years ago.

Famous finds

▲ This mask, discovered in Mycenae, Greece, was believed by Heinrich Schliemann (1822–1890) to belong to the legendary King Agamemnon (born c. 1140 B.C.). It surprised the world because it suggested that a figure from legend might have a basis in historical fact.

All over the world archaeologists are discovering interesting objects that tell them more and more about the past. Usually their discoveries are so specialized that only a handful of scholars and professionals ever get to hear about them. But every once in a while major discoveries are made that are so unusual, rich, or unexpected that they make headline news across the world.

The Sutton Hoo ship burial

In 1939 at Sutton Hoo in Suffolk, England, archaeologists excavating Anglo-Saxon burial mounds made an incredible discovery. They unearthed the remains of a 7th-century A.D. ship, which contained a rich collection of treasures and might have once contained the body of King Raedwald (died A.D. 625). Long ago, when the king died, a ship was hauled out of the water onto dry land. The king's body was placed inside a chamber in the ship, which was loaded with precious objects before being buried. When it was discovered, the timber frame had rotted away, but the treasures still remained.

▶ No definite evidence of a body was discovered at Sutton Hoo, but this magnificent helmet helps us imagine the king. It once would have protected him in battle.

The treasures

The objects inside the ship at Sutton Hoo were in a bad state of preservation, but the treasures give us a rare glimpse into the splendors of the Saxon royal court. Gold jewelry inlaid with colored glass, belt buckles, clasps, shields, helmets, weapons, coins, and drinking horns (all pictured below) hint at the importance and the status of the king.

Similar precious objects were unearthed in 1978 in the grave of a 6th-century B.C. Celtic chief in Hochdorf, Germany. These included drinking horns, weapons, jewelry, and a decorated bronze couch. Elaborate burials, such as those of individuals of high status, help archaeologists understand how earlier societies organized themselves and honored a powerful king or chief who ruled over them.

▶ The Rosetta stone is a polished stone engraved with three versions of the same text, discovered in Egypt in 1799. Later, in 1822, the archaeologist François Champollion (1790–1832) used his knowledge of the ancient Egyptian and ancient Greek languages to decipher the hieroglyphs on the stone. Thousands of other Egyptian hieroglyphs have been decoded since then.

A hidden city

Other headline-grabbing finds include the discovery in 1911 of an entire city that had been hidden for 500 years. Machu Picchu, named after the mountain that rises above it, was a fortified city high up in the Andes of South America (see picture on page 7). It was built by the Incas but was never found by the Spanish who invaded in the 1500s. Its palace, its temple to the Sun, and its elevated location ensured that it became a modern-day wonder of the world.

Nothing too small

Sometimes one fairly small object can have enormous implications for our understanding of the past. The Rosetta stone, for example, revolutionized the way the world understood early Egyptian civilization. It is a stone engraved with three versions of the same text. One was written in ancient Egyptian, one in ancient Greek, and the third in Egyptian picture writing known as hieroglyphs, which no modern person had been able to read. It proved to be a key to this previously mysterious writing system.

▲ Because the Sutton Hoo ship's timber had rotted away over time, all that remained of it was a ghostly imprint in the dirt. However, in this picture, taken at the time of the discovery, the impression left by the wooden hull and even the iron rivets that held the planks together can be seen, giving archaeologists tangible evidence of the scale of the burial.

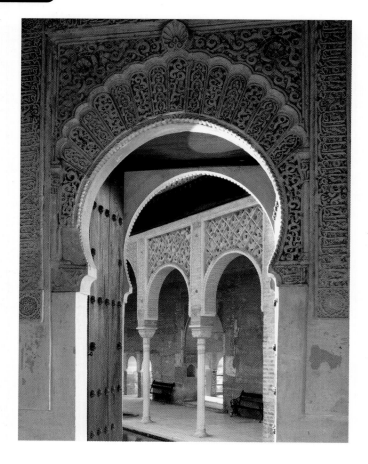

▲ In the A.D. 700s the Moors of North Africa invaded what is now Spain. They were a cultured people who valued fine Architecture, and many of their buildings survive to this day. The Alhambra palace was the last fortress of the Moorish kings of Granada.

▼ In an impressive salvage operation to save the priceless ruins of Pharaoh Ramses II's temples in Abu Simbel from flooding, the statues and columns were sliced into sections and moved to higher ground. They were then reassembled out of the way of the rising water behind the Aswan Dam.

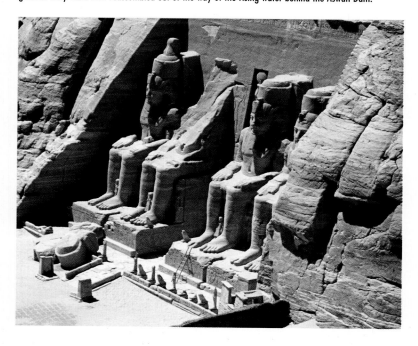

Changing times

Our lives do not stand still for a moment. They are constantly moving and changing in a seri of events. Over thousands of years the amount of change is enormous. Cultures grow and decline, countries go to war and conquer one another, and people develop new technologies and ways of living. The things that people leave behind, in contrast, are motionless and lifeless. In bringing the past back to life it is as if archaeologists are creating a moving image from a series of snapshots.

Change and conquest

Change is rarely sudden. Civilizations rise and fall, and societies build on what went before. Change has often been accompanied by violence as one culture conquers another. For example, the Norman Conquest of England in A.D. 1066 brought huge changes to Anglo-Saxon life, adding new words, architecture, and systems of government to what had gone before. Elsewhere in Europe, for 700 years the Moors of North Africa left their mark on Spain, until they were driven out of their last stronghold of Granada in A.D. 1492.

Difficult choices

Governments often have to choose between saving an archaeological site or developing over it. In 1959 the Egyptian government had to decide whether the building of a dam at Aswan was more important than the preservation of the temples at Abu Simbel, which would have been submerged as the Nile Valley flooded. As a compromise the temples themselves were removed. A similar project is underway to save the Ba Wang temple in China, when a dam due to be completed in 2009 will flood the Chang (Yangtze) river.

War

Throughout history cities have been destroyed by conflict, and the evidence of past battles is all around us. War is not confined to the past and still brings destruction to sites of great archaeological importance. Fighting in the former Yugoslavia in the early 1990s destroyed many ancient and well-loved religious buildings. Possibly the most dramatic act of destruction there took place in Mostar (now in Bosnia) in 1993, when the beautiful 16th-century bridge spanning the river collapsed after months of shelling.

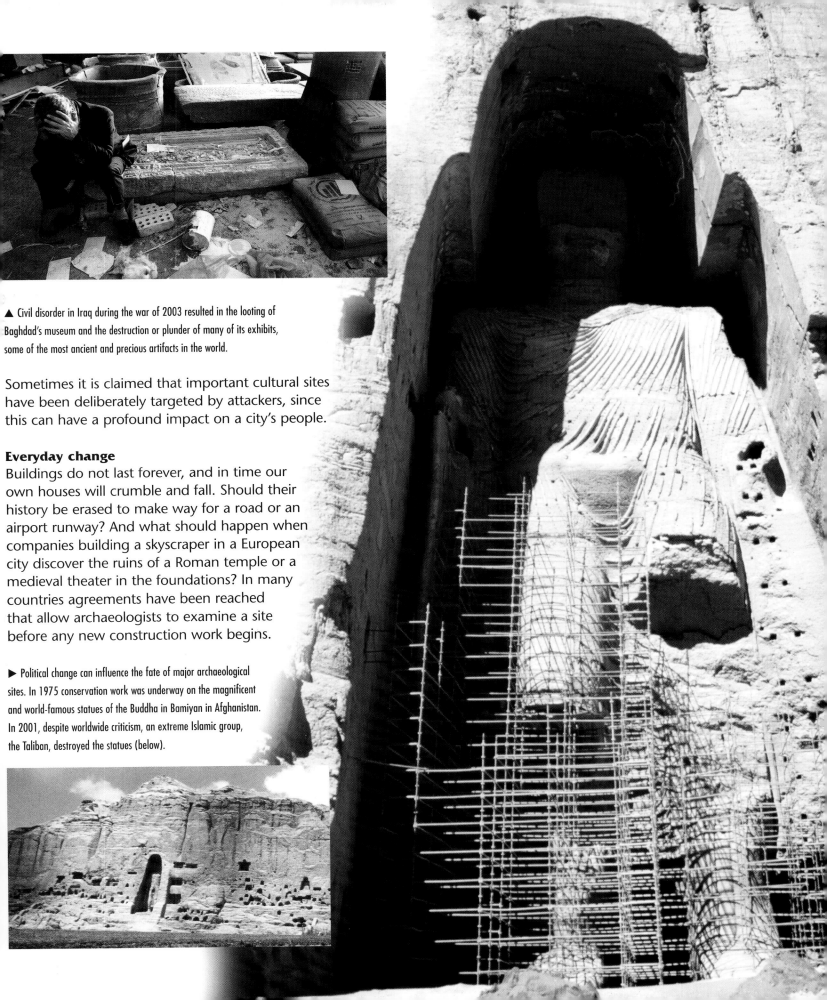

▲ Civil disorder in Iraq during the war of 2003 resulted in the looting of Baghdad's museum and the destruction or plunder of many of its exhibits, some of the most ancient and precious artifacts in the world.

Sometimes it is claimed that important cultural sites have been deliberately targeted by attackers, since this can have a profound impact on a city's people.

Everyday change

Buildings do not last forever, and in time our own houses will crumble and fall. Should their history be erased to make way for a road or an airport runway? And what should happen when companies building a skyscraper in a European city discover the ruins of a Roman temple or a medieval theater in the foundations? In many countries agreements have been reached that allow archaeologists to examine a site before any new construction work begins.

▶ Political change can influence the fate of major archaeological sites. In 1975 conservation work was underway on the magnificent and world-famous statues of the Buddha in Bamiyan in Afghanistan. In 2001, despite worldwide criticism, an extreme Islamic group, the Taliban, destroyed the statues (below).

Where next?

Archaeologists are discovering more about the past all the time. Every day new objects are discovered, and new sites are excavated. But archaeology is not only about collecting more things. It is about extending the boundaries of what we know about the past. It involves everything from improving methods of measuring to developing new theories; from exploring new methods of finding, examining, and storing evidence to displaying it in exciting ways.

▲ The prehistoric cave paintings in Lascaux in southwestern France attracted so many visitors in the decades after their discovery in A.D. 1940 that the images were under threat from changes in temperature, humidity, and even the chemicals in people's breath! In order to preserve them, the cave was closed to the public in 1963, and a full-scale replica, known as Lascaux II, was built nearby as a visitor attraction.

▼ Medical technology is a helpful tool for archaeological research. This Egyptian mummy is being X-rayed in a circular body scanner, enabling the body to be studied without damaging or unwrapping the mummy.

Who owns the past?

In the 1700s and 1800s rich Europeans excavated foreign sites and removed their treasures. Many were scholars with a lot of respect for ancient cultures, and the artifacts were intended for research or public display. But today people are asking whether the objects were theirs to take in the first place. Archaeologists today need to be sensitive to these issues, working closely with governments, museums, and site owners to make sure that accurate records are kept and artifacts are protected. In order to avoid damage to popular sites, visitor numbers may have to be restricted or certain areas closed to the public for protection.

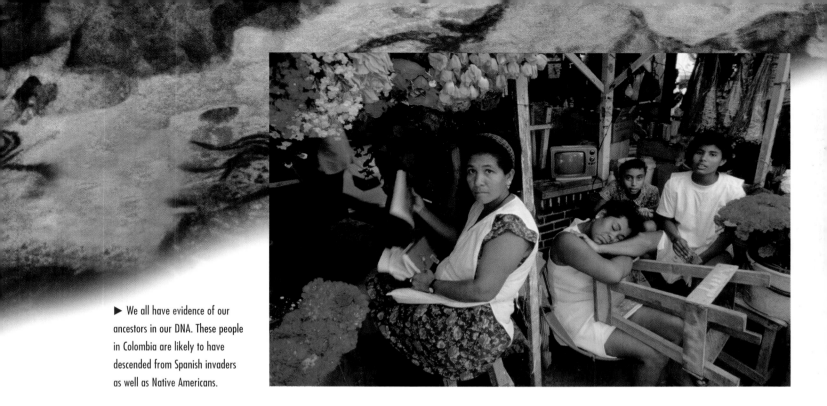

► We all have evidence of our ancestors in our DNA. These people in Colombia are likely to have descended from Spanish invaders as well as Native Americans.

Presentation

Archaeology is not just for archaeologists. It is for all of us. So archaeologists are exploring new ways of presenting their findings to the public. They can use the latest computer graphics to rebuild ancient landscapes in breathtaking detail or to recreate past worlds on television or in movies. Sometimes a historic building is actually rebuilt or restored. For a more hands-on experience museums, such as the Jorvik Viking Centre in York, England, have a type of archaeological theme park, giving visitors the chance to experience the sights, sounds, and even smells of a place in centuries past.

▲ It's not just the distant past that interests archaeologists—and the public. Here visitors to the National Railway Museum in York, England, prepare to take a ride on a working reconstruction of George Stephenson (1781–1848)'s *Rocket*—one of the earliest steam trains, which made its first trip in 1829.

New technology

Developments in science and technology mean that archaeologists have constantly improving tools at their disposal for examining evidence of the past. Improvements in the quality of satellite imaging, ground-penetrating radar, and scientific dating methods will help reveal more about archaeological sites. The latest chemical and biological techniques allow scientists to uncover tiny details of everyday life—pollen grains in household waste or in the long-decayed contents of a person preserved in a peat bog, for example, can tell us a lot about their diet and environment. Scientists can even study the traces of fat left in an ancient pot and figure out which foods were cooked in it.

Archaeologists can use DNA testing to find out if groups of bodies found together are related. They can even study today's people to understand past mysteries. In Colombia DNA research has shown that today's population is mostly descended from European men and Native American women. This suggests that when the Spanish conquered the region, they killed the local men and married the local women. This also supports contemporary evidence of a massacre.

Our recent past

Archaeologists today are excavating remains of the much more recent past. The 1800s produced great inventions and machinery that are now out-of-date. Farm and factory tools made just 100 or 200 years ago may be mysterious to us now. Industrial archaeologists can learn a lot from these objects. They study how changes in transportation and technology affected people's daily lives.

SUMMARY OF CHAPTER 1: WHAT IS ARCHAEOLOGY?

Digging for the past

Archaeology is the study of the physical remains of the past. As we have seen, it involves many different skills. Working on a dig and excavating a site, for example, can be physically difficult, time-consuming work. Both the site and the artifacts have to be analyzed carefully and scientifically. Archaeology also requires intellectual skill and imagination. As their starting point archaeologists take the material remains of individuals, communities, cultures, and whole civilizations and then use this to ask important questions about the past. How did people—whose faces we have never seen except maybe in frescoes or mosaics and whose names we will never know—live their lives? And how have those lives shaped our own?

The Battersea shield, an elaborate Iron Age artifact found in London, England, dating from 350–50 B.C.

Displaying and explaining

Instead of collecting (or even plundering!) artifacts for their own personal satisfaction, archaeologists are responsible for sharing their discoveries with the world. They carefully preserve sites and objects for future generations and display their findings in imaginative ways. Where to display them can sometimes be controversial. Should artifacts be removed and displayed out of their original context in museums? In the case of aboriginal artifacts from Australia aborigines have said no and have asked for the return of their cultural heritage. Many other artifacts are the subject of debates about ownership and about how precious objects should be preserved.

Archaeologists are constantly turning their attention to new places and discovering even more about familiar places. Their purpose is to unearth the objects with sensitivity and, in the process, to add little by little to our wealth of knowledge. Possibly the greatest excitement of all is knowing that there are more treasures waiting to be found, more mysteries waiting to be explained, and more stories waiting to be told.

Go further . . .

 Dig out more information about archaeology: www.digonsite.com

Learn about British digs with Time Team: www.channel4.com/timeteam

Awesome Archaeology by Nick Arnold (Scholastic, 2001)

Archaeology: Discovering the Past by John Orna-Ornstein (Oxford University Press, 2002)

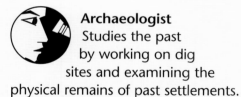 **Archaeologist**
Studies the past by working on dig sites and examining the physical remains of past settlements.

Forensic scientist
Uses the latest scientific techniques to examine ancient human remains.

Historian
Reads and writes about people, places, and events from the past.

Tour guide
Accompanies visitors around archaeological sites.

Volunteer
Helps local archaeologists with their excavation and conservation work.

 Visit the British Museum to see artifacts, including the Sutton Hoo hoard and the Rosetta stone: London, England WC1B 3DG
Phone: 44 020 7323 8482
www.thebritishmuseum.ac.uk

Take a trip back in time to a Viking town at the Jorvik Viking Centre: York, England YO1 9WT
Phone: 44 01904 643 211
www.jorvik-viking-centre.co.uk

See the replica cave paintings from Lascaux II in Montignac, France: www.culture.gouv.fr/culture/arcnat/lascaux/en/

Detail from the "Standard of Ur" (peace side), c. 2600 B.C.

Touching the past

There are hundreds of thousands of archaeological sites in the world. Each one of them adds to our understanding of the past. But some stand out from the rest. They may be very old, like the remains of Catal Hüyük in Turkey, for example, which gave us a clearer picture of life in prehistoric times; or extremely rich in detail, like the ruins of Pompeii; or they may be places, like some battlefield sites

where archaeology challenges existing views of history. Some sites are simply spectacular—such as the tomb of Tutankhamen in Egypt, which amazed the world with its treasures. You can look in detail at a selection of outstanding sites in this chapter. One day you, too, may visit some of the sites and, like archaeologists before you, experience the thrill of touching fragments of the past with your own hands

◀ Tools and weapons, like this flint arrowhead from the Paleolithic period, developed over millions of years. Dating them accurately is extremely difficult because the Paleolithic, or early Stone Age, stretches from two million years ago to around 13,000 years ago. The refinement and precision of this arrowhead, from Slovakia in Europe, suggests a date closer to the end of this period.

● Little Bighorn

● Cahokia

Tenochtitlán ●

Sites around the world

All over the world there are places where people have lived, worked, built homes and cities, fought battles, practiced religion, made art, and buried their dead. There are thousands of archaeological sites full of evidence of the past. The map on this page shows the places that you can explore in the rest of this chapter.

Before settlements

For the earliest people life was a constant struggle for survival. There were no luxuries—only the necessities of food, water, clothing, and shelter. For thousands of years people were nomadic, moving from place to place in order to hunt for animals and gather berries and nuts. We know them as hunter-gatherers. Some of them made their homes in caves. The artifacts that have survived from these times include tools and weapons (such as axes and arrowheads), carved ornaments, jewelry, and very few remains of buildings.

The first settlements

The first farmers settled almost 10,000 years ago in the Middle East. Communities chose where to live and built permanent houses. Similar developments happened slightly later elsewhere. Gradually, all over the world sophisticated civilizations arose—first in Egypt, Mesopotamia, and China. Later settlements developed in Europe, Peru, and east Africa. As civilizations have risen and fallen, they have left behind the wealth of fascinating material evidence that archaeologists study today.

◀ Before people made permanent settlements they lived a nomadic lifestyle, wandering from place to place. Little remains of the temporary homes they built, but early rock art depicting things of importance, like this 10,000-year-old collection of hunting drawings from Namibia in Africa, has survived. Similar cave paintings exist on every continent.

▶ Ceremonial buildings, like the royal mausoleum carved out of the cliffs of the desert, are all that remain of the city of Petra, Jordan, which was at the height of its power between 50 B.C. and A.D. 70. It has provided archaeologists with a wealth of information. Many cultures flourished in the Middle East at this time, and Petra was at the center of important trading routes.

Ring of Brodgar

Newgrange

Vilnius

London

Mary Rose

Verdun

Carnac

Slovakia

Pompeii

Xi'an

Harappa
Mohenjo-Daro

Angkor

Ife and Benin

Athens

Mycenae

Knossos

Catal Hüyük

Great Zimbabwe

Babylon

Petra

Ur

Namibia

Valley of the Kings

▲ This boat, discovered buried alongside the dead ruler in the royal cemeteries of Ur in Mesopotamia (modern-day Iraq), is more than 4,500 years old. Mesopotamian city-states, such as Ur, saw the first blossoming of civilization as we know it. The development of writing in the region put Ur at an archaeological crossroad where history and prehistory overlap.

Catal Hüyük

▲ This terra-cotta figurine of a large woman is believed to be a fertility symbol, representing a "mother goddess" who was worshiped for the rich harvests she could bring to the people.

For thousands of years people lived a nomadic lifestyle. Then, around 9,000 years ago, the hunter-gatherers began to choose where they wanted to live and to build structures in which the whole community could lead more settled lives. Catal Hüyük, in modern-day Turkey, is one of the earliest of these towns, and it gives us a fascinating glimpse into the lives of men and women who first began to domesticate their surroundings so long ago.

The discovery

In 1961 British archaeologist James Mellaart (born 1925) traveled to southern Turkey to excavate an artificial earth mound (*hüyük* in Turkish) that he had discovered three years earlier while surveying the Konya Plain of Anatolia. As he and his team removed layer after layer of soil, they found the remains of a Stone Age town, which had been home to between 5,000 and 6,000 people around 6000 B.C. The site covered an area around the same size as 50 soccer fields and would, at its height, have been one of the most densely populated places on Earth.

◄ The bull, featured in many wall paintings, is a male image of fertility. Fertility was vital to a community that relied on agriculture and hunting for its survival and prosperity. Hunting was important for the food and skins it provided and for the shared ritual it offered the people of the town.

A farming community

Mellaart's excavations (and later ones) unearthed evidence of a highly advanced farming community. The region was fertile at this time, and the people of Catal Hüyük made full use of nature's bounty. Evidence discovered on the site shows that they cultivated cereals, grew grapes and apples, ate chickpeas, lentils, and pistachio nuts, raised sheep and cattle, and hunted wild boars, goats, and deer. They even kept pet dogs to guard their homes.

Urban life

Although Catal Hüyük is the oldest and largest example of an urban settlement, it does not resemble a town in the modern sense. The mud-brick houses were laid out in a large cluster, and there were no streets— and no front doors. People entered their houses from their roofs. Rooms were small, and their plaster walls were often decorated with paintings showing hunting or farming scenes. Catal Hüyük's residents were some of the first people in the world to produce fabrics, wooden bowls, and even mirrors. They also traded goods with other communities from miles away. Fertility symbols were important, and they probably believed in some sort of life after death—the dead were buried beneath the floors of houses with objects they would have used in life such as pots, beads, and bracelets.

▲ This reconstruction of a group of houses in Catal Hüyük shows neat houses, packed closely together. There were no windows or streets, and people entered their houses through the roofs.

▼ This aerial view of what Catal Hüyük could have looked like shows the mud-brick houses tightly packed together. Surrounding the town was a fertile plain—very different from today—with wide areas of marshes that flooded easily and areas inhabited by horses, deer, and wild boars.

Giant stones of western Europe

Eternal monuments to the dead or meeting places for the living? Astronomical calculators or celestial clocks? Boundary stones to mark land ownership or religious shrines to prepare people for the next life? Maybe we will never know for sure why prehistoric peoples throughout western Europe built their mysterious, giant stone monuments, thousands of which cover the landscape. But we do know that their haunting power to fascinate has not diminished—even after 5,000 years.

▲ At Newgrange there are several large stones intricately decorated with patterns such as these spirals. Above the doorway you can see the "roof box" through which the Sun's rays shine along the passage during midwinter.

The passage grave at Newgrange

The prehistoric stone structure at Newgrange in Ireland, built around 3000 B.C., is one of the most famous in western Europe. The passage grave consists of a large stone and turf mound containing a passage that leads to a burial chamber. Like many other prehistoric stone arrangements, the whole structure at Newgrange is precisely aligned so that something special happens at a certain time of the year. At Newgrange on the shortest day of the year (known as the winter solstice) the rising Sun shines directly along the passage, illuminating the wall of the burial chamber.

The mystery

Each winter solstice, for a brief period of around 17 minutes, the dawn rays of the midwinter Sun— in perfect alignment with the passage and the burial chamber—shine light into the darkness. This does not happen by chance. Human beings designed it to happen this way. Why? Does it symbolize that the winter will soon give way to the spring? Or something more—a belief that light and life will triumph over darkness and death? No written records exist to help us decide. That is the mystery of Newgrange.

◄ The 27 standing stones of the Ring of Brodgar in Orkney, Scotland, form part of a complex of ritual structures. Also in Orkney is a wonderfully preserved village of stone houses from the same period (3100–2500 B.C.).

◄ The circular mound at Newgrange is around 312 ft. (95m) in diameter and 49 ft. (15m) high and is made up of 200,000 tons of stones and dirt. It has been estimated that it would have taken 80 men four days to carry just one four-ton stone from the closest quarry, so it was a huge construction feat. The white quartz stone facade, which shines dazzlingly at the winter solstice, was restored in the 1960s.

Eternally fascinating

These massive stones are also called megaliths—from the Greek words *mega*, meaning large, and *lithos*, meaning stone. People have always been fascinated by them, their locations, and why they were built. The stones were transported across large distances for no obvious practical purpose, so it seems that they must have had great importance in communities' rituals or religious lives. It was only in the 1950s that archaeologists realized that they dated back to between 3000 and 1500 B.C. As new finds come to light, they are building up a more complete picture of the people who lived with them.

The big questions

The megaliths may have been temples, places of ceremony or sacrifice, or giant calendars for recording the seasons. We can be sure that these monuments were built with life's big questions in mind—how we fit into the pattern of the universe, who or what controls our lives, and what awaits us after death. Many were built to house the dead, and the importance of funeral rites was enormous. Objects unearthed in burial mounds suggest that people in these early societies believed that death was not the end of things but instead that it was part of a longer journey.

▲ The passage in the burial chamber at Newgrange, dazzlingly lit up by the midwinter Sun, must have been an amazing sight for those who witnessed it in prehistoric times. Rediscovered in A.D. 1699, it is still magnificent today.

► At Carnac in Brittany, France, there are stone alignments made up of 3,000 megaliths, stretching for several miles. They might have been used as a place of worship. They might also have been devices to track the changing patterns of the sky in a society where climate and the seasons were important.

Harappa and Mohenjo-Daro

Close to the cities of Lahore and Hyderabad in modern-day Pakistan stand the ruins of two of the earliest and greatest prehistoric brick cities built along the Indus Valley around 2700 B.C. These cities were part of a major Bronze Age civilization. Forgotten and neglected for centuries, they were first excavated by archaeologists in the 1920s.

▲ Some archaeologists have suggested that the ordered grid pattern of the streets and houses of the Indus Valley cities (seen here at Mohenjo-Daro) is the earliest attempt at organized town planning. Excavations have revealed that almost every house was connected to both sewers and a water supply.

Harappa

When archaeologists started to excavate the site at Harappa, they found the remains of a remarkable city. It had been built in an organized grid pattern with houses at right angles to each other. In 1921 they unearthed evidence of a massive citadel (stronghold or fortress) that looked down on the residential quarters and that had contained public buildings, such as workshops and a large grain-storing structure, which, to the people of the city, served as a type of central bank.

Cities of traders

The merchants of the Indus Valley established links with surrounding peoples—even as far away as modern-day Iraq—by trading timber, precious stones, gold, and ivory. In Harap the goods were stored in warehouses, where archaeologists have discovered many clay seals of guarantee, which would have identified particular merchants. Terra-cotta models of distinctive two-wheeled carts have also been found, giving an indication of how goods were transported overland.

▲ Sir Mortimer Wheeler (1890–1976) was one of the first archaeologists to divide a site into distinct sections. He carried out detailed excavations in the Indus Valley in the 1950s.

▼ This reconstruction of the citadel at Harappa shows the houses arranged in tiers above each other in order to maximize light and space. Notice that the city has massive ramparts (barriers) with thick walls to protect the population during times of flood.

▲ The abundance of mud from the Indus floodplain provided the raw material for the brick structures of the earliest cities. It also allowed potters to perfect their craft, producing beautiful painted pots like this one above, found at Mohenjo-Daro.

Mohenjo-Daro

The excavation of Mohenjo-Daro added to the emerging image of the Indus Valley civilization. Meaning "the mound of the dead," Mohenjo-Daro was around one square mile (2.6km²), and at its peak (c. 2000 B.C.) it housed 35,000 people. Archaeologists discovered a large bathhouse in the citadel, which was thought to be the focus of religious rituals, as well as figurines thought to represent a mother goddess.

Decline

In their heyday Harappa and Mohenjo-Daro were thriving communities where people lived in luxury and comfort. No one knows for sure why these once magnificent cities fell into decline, but it is clear that by around 1700 B.C. they had been abandoned. One reason might be that by this time the Indus river had significantly changed its course. Its life-giving waters, the source of the cities' agricultural prosperity, had retreated. Other causes could have been an outbreak of disease or colonization by the Aryan people of central Asia. Whatever the explanation, the first great civilization of the Indian subcontinent had come to an end.

▲ This ornate gold and silver double ring for holding oxen reins was found in the royal graves of Ur.

Ur and Babylon

Mesopotamia, in the "fertile crescent" of land bounded by the Tigris and Euphrates rivers (in modern-day Iraq), has been called the birthplace of civilization. It was in this place around 5,000 years ago that the Sumerians, Assyrians, and Babylonians built great cities and laid the foundations of magnificent civilizations. Archaeologists have put together a fascinating picture of these places.

The Sumerian city of Ur

Ur, one of the oldest cities in Mesopotamia, was at its peak from 2100 to 2000 B.C. Writing was first developed there. Its remains were discovered in A.D. 1854 when archaeologists found a massive dirt and brick mound at the site. Later excavations revealed a huge step-sided pyramid, known as a ziggurat. This was the centerpiece of the ancient city and was mostly used for worship. At the top was a temple, while at lower levels there were rooms for animal sacrifices and for the preparation of other offerings to the gods.

The royal graves

In 1926, at a cemetery where the ancient kings and queens had been buried, archaeologists discovered a huge array of precious objects—from golden helmets and shields to elaborate musical instruments made in the shape of animals. The graves also contained a grisly secret. A living procession of soldiers, musicians, and servants had accompanied the royal corpses into the tomb. Each one had carried a fatal poison that they would drink once they were inside, ready to accompany their rulers into eternity.

◀ With the discovery of the royal graves at Ur, a wealth of evidence of a rich and sophisticated civilization came to light. Treasures included this necklace worn by Queen Pu-abi of Ur (died c. 2500 B.C.). She was buried in all of her finest belongings, accompanied by 25 attendants who went to their deaths and were buried alongside her.

The rise of Babylon

Over the centuries Ur was gradually overshadowed in Mesopotamia by the city of Babylon, at its height under King Nebuchadrezzar II (ruled 605–562 B.C.). He fortified the city with massive ramparts and built an elaborate blue-glazed brick gate, dedicated to Ishtar, goddess of love. Inside the city walls was the Temple of Marduk, a vast ziggurat modeled on the one at Ur. The king ordered it to be built even higher than Ur's so that it would be a visible symbol of the city's wealth and power.

The Hanging Gardens

Archaeologists have unearthed evidence of glazed bricks used for Babylon's Ishtar Gate, and a reconstruction of it has been built in the Pergamon Museum in Berlin, Germany, complete with decorations based on animals and mythical beasts. The city's most famous structure, however, was a vast artificial mountain displaying a stunning collection of exotic plants, shrubs, and flowers. The Hanging Gardens of Babylon were one of the seven wonders of the ancient world. They have captured people's imagination ever since, although to this day no actual remains have been found.

▼ Nebuchadrezzar II ordered the Temple of Marduk to be built so big that it would "reach up to heaven." Many people think that this could have been the origin of the biblical legend of the Tower of Babel— a tower that was built to try to reach heaven.

▲ The blue Ishtar Gate is the only monument from Babylon that has well-preserved remains. Behind it in this artist's reconstruction is the impressive Temple of Marduk. Step-sided ziggurats, such as this one, were a characteristic feature of the Mesopotamian landscape and symbolized the link between heaven and Earth. Behind it are the magnificent Hanging Gardens.

The Palace of Knossos

Legend tells us that many thousands of years ago, on the Mediterranean island we know today as Crete, there lived a cruel tyrant named King Minos. His fabulous palace contained a labyrinth (an underground maze) guarded by a terrible monster known as the Minotaur, who was half man and half bull. Many stories were told about Minos, the Minotaur, and the labyrinth. But was it ever more than just a story? Could the palace really have existed and the myths have had a basis in historical fact? A 19th-century English archaeologist was convinced that it could.

▲ Sir Arthur Evans was the first person to excavate the Palace of Knossos. He coined the term "Minoan" to describe the rich civilization he unearthed.

Myth into fact

In A.D. 1899 archaeologist Arthur Evans (1851–1941) bought a plot of land in the town of Knossos and began excavations. He discovered the remains of an ornate palace with a maze of corridors and courtyards—and everywhere, in mosaics, frescoes, and statues, there were images of bulls. The story of the labyrinth was written down around 1000 B.C., but the archaeological evidence suggested that the palace had been built at least 1,000 years earlier. Could a real palace, with a network of corridors and with people who revered bulls and enjoyed bull fighting, have inspired a story that was embellished through the generations? Evans thought so.

◀ Bulls were a symbol of male power and fertility in many civilizations of this time. This bull-shaped *rhyton* (ritual pouring vessel used to pour liquids as part of a religious ceremony), comes from Mycenae, the Mediterranean civilization that was to destroy Knossos.

A luxurious life

Evans discovered evidence of a fantastic palace. Its courtyard offered cool spaces, where, in the summer, people could escape from the fierce heat. In the winter under-floor heating kept the palace warm. Sunken baths, running water, and lush gardens all added to the splendor. But it was more than just a royal palace. It was a whole town in miniature, with storerooms, temples, workshops—everything to support a Bronze Age civilization 4,000 years ago.

Minoan civilization

The Minoan civilization was the first great European civilization. Its position at the center of the Mediterranean trade routes was crucial to its success. But the island's wealth attracted the envy of another palace civilization based in Mycenae, to the northwest. From the 1400s B.C. Mycenean warriors began to invade and colonize Crete, signaling the beginning of the end of the Minoan way of life.

▲ The bull was given an honored place in society and was depicted on everything from pottery to wall paintings. There were elaborate games involving young athletes leaping over the bulls' horns and doing handstands on the bulls' backs as the animals charged toward them.

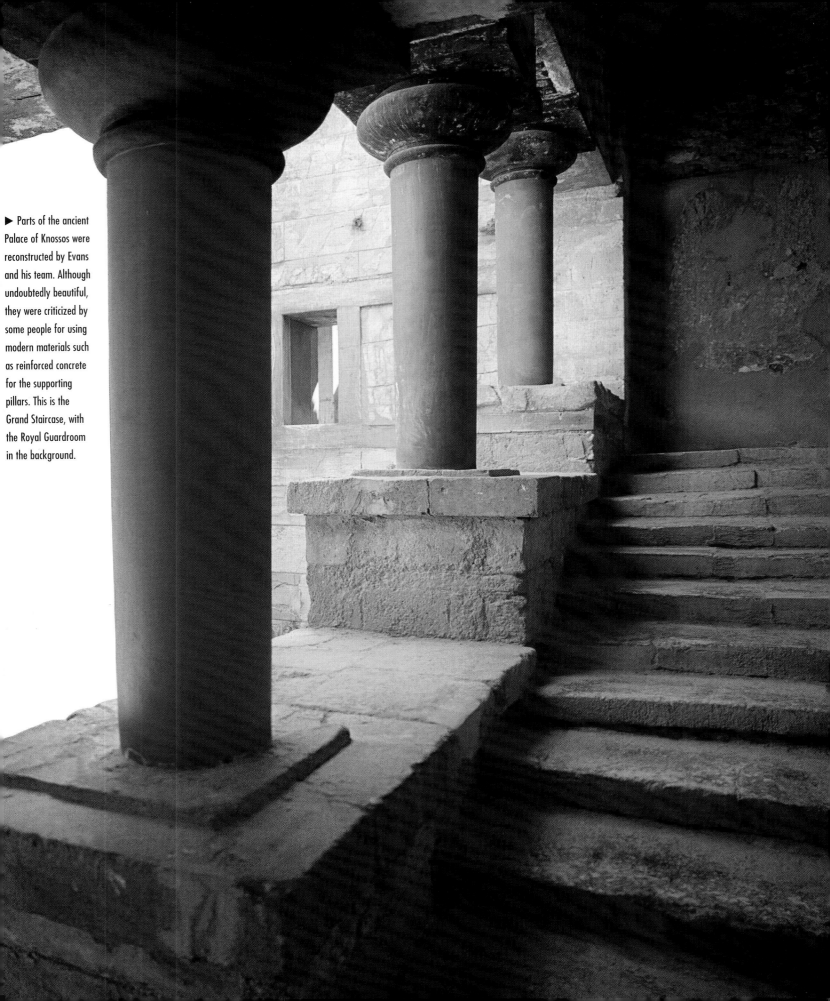

▶ Parts of the ancient Palace of Knossos were reconstructed by Evans and his team. Although undoubtedly beautiful, they were criticized by some people for using modern materials such as reinforced concrete for the supporting pillars. This is the Grand Staircase, with the Royal Guardroom in the background.

The tomb of Tutankhamen

The civilization of the ancient Egyptians lasted for more than 2,000 years, ending around 1000 B.C. They were ruled by pharaohs (kings), and the country is scattered with giant pyramids and elaborate royal tombs, built as monuments to the dead pharaohs and filled with objects for their journeys to the afterlife. One tomb is that of the boy king Tutankhamen (died c. 1400 B.C.). He reigned for a short time, but his tomb, when opened, revealed the most spectacular collection of treasures the world had ever seen.

A preoccupation with death

The Egyptians believed that death was just the next stage in a person's life. They thought that they could only be reborn and live forever if their bodies were preserved. Egyptians preserved their dead as mummies and placed them in sarcophagi (stone coffins). Royal mummies were entombed in burial chambers beneath the desert, often underneath imposing pyramids that symbolized stairways to the stars.

The tombs

The tombs of the Egyptian pharaohs were filled with objects thought to be of use in the afterlife. In many cases grave robbers have looted the tombs and stolen the riches they contained. For many years archaeologists have tried to discover and put on public display artifacts that tell us more about the civilization of ancient Egypt. Howard Carter (1874–1939) was exactly this type of man.

pharaoh's belongings

burial chamber

treasure room and shrine

▲ Tutankhamen's tomb as seen by Howard Carter

▲ As Howard Carter peered into the tomb of Tutankhamen, he experienced the excitement that drives all archaeologists—to see with their own eyes and touch with their own hands objects that have been undiscovered for centuries. It was, he wrote later, "The day of days. The most wonderful that I have ever lived."

A discovery waiting to happen

All over Egypt there are tombs, some of which have yet to reveal their secrets. One of them is that of Hatshepsut one of the few female pharaohs. She ruled for 15 years until her death in 1458 B.C. in place of her nephew, Tuthmosis III (died 1426 B.C.), who was too young to rul After her death Tuthmosis tried to erase her from history by attacking monuments built to her and removing her name from written records. But he left her tomb alone, and it remained intact for centuries, leaving today's archaeologists with even more mysteries to solve.

◄ Possibly the most magnificent of all of he riches in the tomb was the solid gold mask of Tutankhamen, staring out at us across a gulf in history of 3,000 years.

▲ The tomb was a mix of the most amazing artifacts— strange and intriguing objects from an ancient civilization. The dry atmosphere meant that things such as nuts, dried fruits, and funeral flowers had been preserved.

The tomb of Tutankhamen

On November 26, 1922 Carter was on the brink of one of the most exciting discoveries any archaeologist has ever made. He was convinced that he was at the outside of the walled-up tomb of Tutankhamen. He lit a candle and made a hole in the wall. The dead air that had last been breathed n by the pharaoh's servants made the flame flicker, but when his eyes had adjusted to the light, he saw the most wonderful things he had ever seen—chests, statues, musical nstruments, wine jars, clothes, games, mummies, jewels, swords, daggers, and much, much more. Everyday objects or a pharaoh, priceless treasures for the modern world

▲ Hatshepsut's tomb in the Valley of the Kings was discovered by Howard Carter in 1916. In his diaries he describes how he surprised tomb robbers in the entrance and chased them away. The tomb is still being excavated by archaeologists today, and they are finding new things all the time

The Acropolis of Athens

The Acropolis—the citadel that once contained some of the most impressive structures the world has ever seen—dominates the Greek city of Athens. Its ruins are a visible reminder of the achievements of a vanished society that laid down the foundations of Western civilization. The remains are a history in stone of a culture that gave the world politics, mathematics, drama, philosophy, and democracy. It was at the Acropolis that these words took practical shape, contributing to a society that prized beauty, truth, and order above everything else.

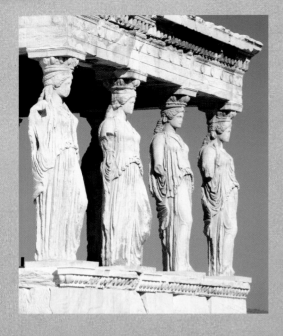

▲ These figures, called Caryatids, support part of the Erechtheum, a temple on the Acropolis built in honor of the goddess Athena, the sea god Poseidon, and Erechtheus, the legendary king of Athens.

▶ The Parthenon dominates the Acropolis. It has had many uses— it became a Christian shrine in the A.D. 400s and an Islamic mosque in the 1400s. Later it was even used for temporary gunpowder storage and was mostly destroyed after an explosion in 1687.

Fortress and shrine

The Acropolis was a natural fortress during times of war and the place in which Athenians conducted their social, political, and religious lives during times of peace. Archaeologists have uncovered evidence that it had been in continuous use as a settlement or shrine since before 650 B.C. During the Classical period (460–330 B.C.) three temples were built on the ruins of earlier ones. The most important is the Parthenon—built by the Athenian statesman Pericles (c. 495–429 B.C.) and dedicated to the city's protecting spirit, the goddess Athena.

The Parthenon

Built from the finest marble and originally brightly painted, the Parthenon became the emblem of classical Greek civilization. Sculpted along the top was a carved frieze depicting a procession that was part of a great four-yearly festival in honor of Athena. By studying its wealth of details, archaeologists can piece together a picture of life, worship, and celebration in Greece in the 400s B.C.

Beyond Athens

There were many other shrines built for the gods and goddesses of ancient Greece. One of the most important was the shrine to Apollo, known as "the bright one," in Delphi. Excavations began in A.D. 1893, and the artifacts that were unearthed showed how the Greeks worshipped Apollo as the light of reason and order—as opposed to the darkness of chaos and ignorance. They also believed Delphi was at the center, or "navel," of the world. There priestesses foretold the future in riddles. Modern geological examination has suggested that they may have made their predictions while in a trancelike state owing to hallucinogenic gases escaping from the rocks.

▼ Part of the Parthenon frieze was removed by Lord Elgin (1766–1841) in the 1800s and sold to the British Museum in London, England, where it has remained for more than 200 years. The Greek government has repeatedly asked for its return and hopes one day to display it near the Acropolis.

The Terra-Cotta Army

▲ Qin Shi Huangdi was a ruthless emperor who imposed his authority violently. Here he is shown executing scholars.

For more than 2,000 years the plains around Mount Li, near present-day Xi'an in China, were hiding an astonishing secret. In 1974, by chance, the secret came to light. What emerged captured the imagination of the world. Peasants digging wells had found fragments of life-size terra-cotta figures of soldiers. Archaeologists were intrigued and started excavating the site. There, in a series of ancient trenches that had laid undisturbed since 200 B.C., was a terra-cotta army of 7,500 full-size warriors, horses, and chariots.

Standing guard

The statues at Mount Li were there to protect China's first emperor, Qin Shi Huangdi (259–210 B.C.), on his journey through the afterlife. Qin Shi Huangdi ruled his people with an iron fist, and he was greatly feared. Even dropping litter in his capital city, Luoyang, could be punished by whipping or by a heavy fine. Yet under his rule the peasants were mostly well-off, thanks to his reforms.

▲ In a field near Xi'an in north-central China stands the burial mound of the emperor. It is rumored to contain fabulous treasures—but also booby traps for those who dare to enter.

◄ Figures in the Terra-Cotta Army are astonishingly lifelike and look as if they really are ready to fight to defend the dead emperor. They were painted in the colors of their platoons, but over time the colors faded to an ash gray.

The emperor's achievements

During his reign Qin Shi Huangdi improved the agricultural and road systems and standardized both the currency and the writing system. His prosperous empire was often targeted for attack—particularly on its northern border—by tribes of nomads. These enemies had no permanent settlements to invade and destroy, so they were impossible to defeat. Instead they had to be kept out. Qin Shi Huangdi famously ordered the construction of the Great Wall of China, a huge defensive barrier. When completed centuries later, the wall stretched for almost 1,550 mi. (2,500km).

▶ Chinese archaeologists slowly and painstakingly uncover a row of statues that had been hidden for more than 2,000 years. They take great care not to damage the statues as they clear away their covering of soil.

Attention to detail

Careful study of the statues showed that no two were the same. Each one had been sculpted from life and showed, in breathtaking detail, what the imperial army of the time would have looked like. The heads and bodies of the soldiers were hollow, but their legs were solid in order to bear the weight. Just as they had served the emperor in life, so they guarded his tomb and were believed to protect him in death. For this they had been armed with real weapons. Amazingly when Chinese archaeologists examined them, they found that many of the blades were still sharp enough to cut through flesh.

The riddle of the tomb

Although the burial pits with their vast model army have been excavated, these are just part of a vast necropolis (city of the dead) inside Mount Li, which also includes a palace and temple. The emperor's tomb itself has so far been left untouched. There are rumors that it contains fantastic treasures—rivers of mercury, gold and silver statues, ornaments made out of jade and precious stones, and much much more. But there are also rumors that within the tomb lie great dangers—lethal booby traps and crossbows primed 2,000 years ago, aimed and ready to fire at anyone bold enough to disturb the great ruler's final earthly resting place.

▶ Qin Shi Huangdi began preparing for his life in the afterworld long before his death in 210 B.C. Historical sources tell us that more than 700,000 men were drafted to build the burial mound. Surrounding the tomb are at least four large pits containing terra-cotta warriors. Pit number one, shown here, contains 3,200 soldiers. The figures were modeled on the imperial army and include cavalrymen, infantrymen, archers, and charioteers.

Pompeii

▲ The smallest details of Pompeian life remain, from these eggs and eggshells to loaves of bread probably baked on the day of the eruption and carbonized in the heat.

For the Romans in Pompeii, August 24, A.D. 79 began like any other day. As they woke up, no one could have known that their lives would soon be ending and their city buried under volcanic ash. Mount Vesuvius erupted only hours later, firing molten lava and rock that rained down on the city. The terrified inhabitants were buried wherever they fell, suffocated by the heat. But the layers of ash that shrouded the city also preserved it, freezing it in time for more than 1,700 years.

Opening the time capsule

The systematic excavation of Pompeii and nearby Herculaneum (which suffered a similar fate) began around A.D. 1860. Colorful wall paintings that came to light from beneath the dust show the luxury enjoyed by the well-to-do Roman citizens. They shopped in market stalls overflowing with fruits, vegetables, and fish; they wore fine fabrics; they lived in stylish houses—many of them built around an elegant central courtyard.

Entertainment

The public buildings that have been excavated in Pompeii show that the people had a passion for public spectacles and entertainment of every type. In the *paelestra,* or gymnasium, for example, they could watch sports competitions, while in the nearby amphitheater there were bloody contests between gladiators and wild beasts. They could watch plays in the theater or go to the public baths, where they could gossip about the details of their lives.

▼ Ruins, such as these of the House of the Faun, let us see inside the actual homes of the Pompeians. In the foreground is an elaborate marble floor.

◀ This poignant plaster cast of an inhabitant in the last moments of his or her life gives us an idea of the terror of the people as they crouched on the ground, desperately hoping to escape the lethal dust and heat.

▶ In this aerial view of Pompeii today you can see the imposing outline of Mount Vesuvius in the background, looming over the town.

Statues of fear

The last minutes of the lives of Pompeii's inhabitants were terrible beyond belief. The Roman writer Pliny the Younger, staying nearby at the time, wrote of the destruction, "You could hear the screams of the women and babies and the cries of the men. There were some who prayed for death and others who prayed for help from the gods." It seemed as if the world had been plunged into darkness forever. Archaeologists have made these final dreadful moments vivid by pouring plaster into the holes left by the bodies in the volcanic dust, producing remarkable statues of men, women, children, and animals.

A snapshot of a vast empire

Pompeii and Herculaneum are the most extensive urban excavations ever completed. They tell us an incredible amount about all aspects of life in those tragic cities. All over Europe and North Africa there are thousands of other Roman remains—Pompeii helps us understand these a little more.

▲ Throughout their empire the Romans built thriving towns like Pompeii. Great feats of engineering made this possible—this aqueduct, the Pont du Gard in France, is one example. Aqueducts supplied the inhabitants of Roman towns with a reliable, plentiful water supply.

Angkor Wat

In the 500 years between the A.D. 800s and 1300s much of Southeast Asia was ruled by the Khmer, a Hindu people whose capital city was Angkor. Its kings, who were also believed to be gods, constructed elaborate temples in the jungles of modern-day Cambodia and Thailand as visible reminders of the link between humankind and the spirit world. The most dramatic of these temples was Angkor Wat.

Symbols of eternity

King Suryavarman II (reigned A.D. 1113–1150) wanted to build the most elaborate temple the empire had ever seen. He constructed Angkor Wat as an earthly reflection of Mount Meru, the place in Hindu legend believed to be the home of the gods. Angkor Wat's five ornately carved towers represent the five peaks of the holy mountain, and they would have filled ordinary people with a sense of awe as they approached this sacred place.

◀ This stone head is just part of an astonishing display of carvings in Angkor. Archaeologists have discovered that the carvings that run along the outer walls of the temple make up the largest continuous frieze in the world, depicting stories from Hindu mythology.

▼ Imagine the excitement of finding this magnificent temple, hidden by overgrown jungle vegetation. This is what happened in A.D. 1860, when a French botanist "rediscovered" Angkor. The Khmer empire had been forgotten by the rest of the world since its collapse in the A.D. 1200s. This remarkable find meant the splendor of the Khmer empire came to light once again.

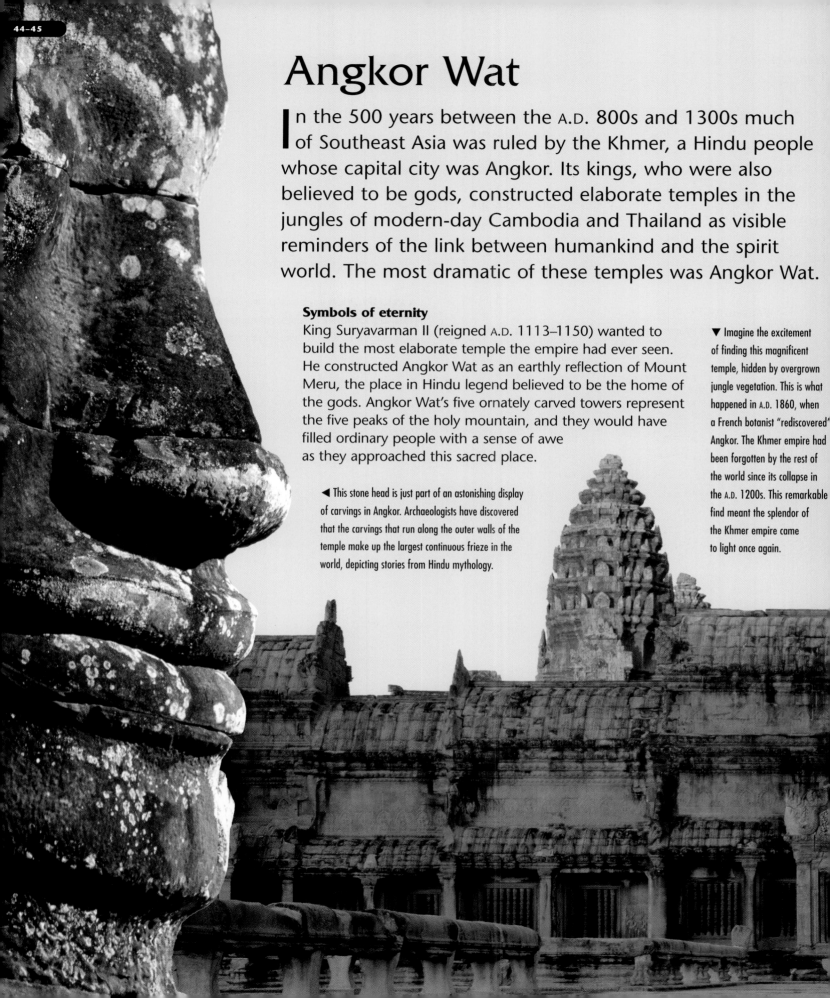

A model of the universe

The city of Angkor was crisscrossed by a complex network of irrigation channels that supplied drinking water to the people and watered the surrounding rice fields. The main compound was surrounded by a giant moat and approached by a causeway, whose balustrades were carved in the shape of serpents representing the fertility of the universe. The canal system was designed to be practical and to reflect the religious belief that Mount Meru was surrounded by a huge ocean. Archaeologists have taken precise measurements of the temple and have shown that it was built to symbolize the movements of the Sun and the Moon. As such, Angkor Wat is modeled on the universe itself.

▲ Angkor Wat is a huge temple complex, surrounded by walls and a moat 590-ft. (180-m)-wide and 2.5-ft. (4-km)-long. The temple is modeled on the universe itself and represents, in fixed stone, the movement of the heavens. The inner holy sanctum and its five ornate central towers are clearly visible in this aerial view.

Everyday life

The temple carvings also tell us a lot about the everyday lives of the Khmer people. They show them at work and at play, preparing food, hunting, or tending their animals. Evidence from the site shows that the central complex was used as a religious and administrative headquarters, housing the royal family and the court. Peasants lived in the fields beyond in bamboo huts built on stilts. They would have supported their families with livestock raised on their their domestic plots.

A people at war

The Khmer civilization came at a price. Their supremacy in the region depended on the force of the army, and the temple carvings show kings and soldiers going into battle on elephants equipped for fighting. Their tusks were armed with sharp metal points designed to inflict maximum damage on the enemy at the same time as archers sitting on the elephants' backs would unleash a lethal volley of arrows into the opposing army. These vivid scenes of battle carved onto the silent stone are all that remain to portray a once powerful empire.

Cahokia

One thousand years ago hunters traveling along what we now know as the central Mississippi river valley would have come across an extraordinary sight. Rising up from the flat plains all around them was a collection of neatly organized timber and mud houses with a giant, 98-ft. (30-m) -tall mound towering above the center. To the weary travelers it would have looked like a modern-day metropolis— which, in its own way, it was.

▲ Before the Mississippian culture developed an earlier Native American culture called the Hopewell culture flourished in the region between 200 B.C. and A.D. 500. This Hopewell stone ornament has a distinctive hand symbol.

A trading people

Cahokia was the most sophisticated prehistoric settlement north of Mexico, and at its peak (around A.D. 1100–1250) it was home to between 10,000 and 20,000 people. Merchants traveling long distances helped spread the so-called Mississippian culture over a large area, from the Gulf coast in the south to the Great Lakes in the north and the Atlantic coast in the east to what is now Oklahoma in the west.

Daily life

In its heyday Cahokia was full of life. Men and women farmed the land, growing pumpkins, sunflowers, and corn, while others fished and hunted in order to provide the community with food. When they were not at work, they enjoyed singing and dancing and, as archaeological evidence has shown, playing dice games.

The settlement was ruled by a chief who was believed to be the brother of the Sun and gifted with spiritual powers. Less important were members of his family. Trusted friends also had some authority. Together these people formed an elite (superior) class separate from everyone else.

The great stockade

At the heart of the settlement was a 10-ft. (3-km) -long wooden stockade (protective fence). For a long time archaeologists thought that this had a purely social function, screening off the elite and wealthy from everyone else. Examination has shown that it was primarily used as a defensive structure to protect the settlement against attacks.

▲ Great Serpent Mound in Ohio is the country's finest so-called effigy mound, built around 2,000 years ago. No skeletons have been found there, which suggests that it was not a burial place but instead a ritual structure. The ripples in the snake's back are aligned with the rays of the Sun at important times of the year.

The mounds

The most distinctive feature of the Cahokia settlement is its series of more than 100 dirt mounds. The exact purpose of these is not clear, although some were used for burial purposes and others to support houses raised up off of the ground. The largest mound, known as Monk's Mound, is located at the heart of the settlement and towers above it. At the top sacred fires burned all day and all night in honor of the gods. There are other, smaller mound settlements in the area. In Moundville, Alabama, the burial mounds have been found to be especially rich in artifacts.

▼ Cahokia's houses were arranged in rows around an open plaza (square). They had pitched roofs with magnificent carved animal heads at the top. In its day the settlement was one of the continent's great urban centers. It contained not only ordinary homes but also structures for communal use such as meeting halls, grain storehouses, and saunalike sweat lodges.

Kingdoms of West Africa

People who visit the bustling industrial town of Ife in Nigeria in Africa may be unaware of a hidden city beneath their feet. For hundreds of years it has slowly been slipping out of sight, buried under successive layers of new buildings. But if the ruins of that ancient city could speak, they would tell tales of a great civilization that flourished for more than 300 years from the A.D. 1100s. Ife and nearby Benin were the centers of important forest kingdoms in western Africa at this time. These sites are rich in artifacts, which allow the past to speak to us today.

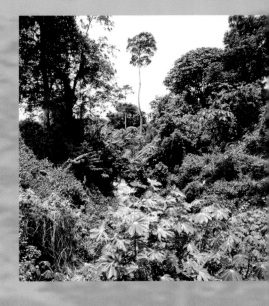

▲ Nature moves quickly to swallow up any evidence of the past. Here the ruins of the ancient city of Benin and its 13th-century fortifications have been overgrown by dense vegetation.

A religious capital

Ife was the capital of the Yoruba kingdom, the spiritual homeland of a nation whose rulers were believed to be gods. According to tradition, it was founded around A.D. 1300 by Oduduwa, the first mythological oni, or king, of Ife. When a king died, exquisitely crafted masks bearing his likeness were cast out of iron, copper, or bronze and carried in the air by the people who believed he would continue to help them overcome difficulties in their lives. Many of these beautiful and mysterious artifacts survive today.

Daily life

The people of Ife and Benin made their living herding cattle and growing crops in the fertile grasslands of western Africa. Oil from cultivated palm trees was used not only for cooking but also for offering to Ogun, the warrior god of metalworking. Shrines to Ogun have been discovered in the royal palace in Ife, along with masks depicting the trickster spirit Eshu, the gods' messenger. The sculptures of kings, queens, gods, and goddesses show these kingdoms had a complex, highly developed religious and artistic culture.

▶ When Portuguese explorers arrived in West Africa in the 1400s, Ife was in decline, eclipsed by the neighboring kingdoms of Benin and Oyo. Masks, like this one from Benin, depicted gods and kings and were an expression of the power and mystery of the royal court. They were sometimes placed on altars during religious rituals or worn as part of court ceremonies.

◀ In this bronze plaque, discovered in the royal palace in Benin, the oba, or king, is shown with two warriors bearing lances at his sides. The kingship of Benin was related to that of Ife—the oba of Benin was traditionally thought to be a descendant of Oduduwa, the founder of Ife. Both cities had elaborate royal palaces and shrines.

▲ Gertrude Caton-Thompson (A.D. 1888–1985) began excavations in Great Zimbabwe in 1929. She proved that this had been a major site of African culture in the A.D. 1000s to 1300s.

Great Zimbabwe

At the same time hundreds of miles to the southeast of Ife and Benin there was another remarkable civilization that has fascinated archaeologists. The ruins of Great Zimbabwe, a massive stone enclosure, or "zimbabwe," that once housed a palace city, were systematically excavated in the early 1900s by British archaeologist Gertrude Caton-Thompson. At the time many Europeans thought that this African culture had been influenced by European—especially Portuguese—explorers and travelers. Her research on objects she excavated at the site told a different story.

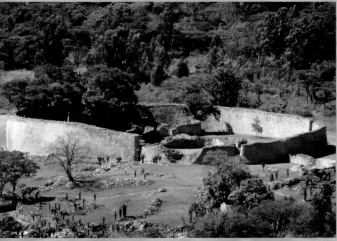

▲ The stone-walled enclosure of Great Zimbabwe is the largest and most impressive of several similar enclosures in southeast Africa. For many years the question of who built it remained a mystery. It is now thought to have been built by the Shona people.

The Aztecs' great temple

▲ The Aztecs did not record their history in writing as we know it but in a system of pictures in books called codices. Many show the Templo Mayor and the ritual sacrifices performed there.

The Aztecs settled in present-day Mexico in the 1100s following the collapse of the earlier Toltec civilization. In the early 1300s they founded the city of Tenochtitlán, built on an island in a lake. Within 400 years they had conquered many peoples and built up a rich, strong, and fearsome empire. At the center of the empire was Tenochtitlán. At the center of the city—and at the heart of city life— was the Aztecs' great temple, the Templo Mayor.

The sacred city

The heart of Tenochtitlán was its sacred plaza, an area of temples and pyramids used for worshiping the gods of rain, fire, wind, Sun, and war. Dominating the plaza was the Templo Mayor, with two temples on top—to the rain god Tlaloc and the Sun god Huitzilopochtli. The Aztecs believed that every night Huitzilopochtli left the sky and battled with the forces of the night. If he was killed, the Sun would never rise again. So each night he had to be strengthened—with blood from human sacrifices.

◄ This incense burner is in the shape of the rain god Tlaloc. In an agricultural society that relied on sunshine and rainfall to ripen its crops, the worship of gods of the elements was very important.

Rise and fall

Rumors of Tenochtitlán's wealth spread far and wide. Stories were told of its markets, harvests, jewelry, and ornaments. In A.D. 1519 these tales of riches attracted the Spanish conquistador (soldier-adventurer) Hernando Cortez (1485–1547). What he and his small army saw as they approached the city took their breath away—a dazzling vista of buildings surrounded by a clear, blue lake. For awhile Cortez and the Aztec emperor, Montezuma II (1480–1520), got along well. But later the strangers laid siege to Tenochtitlán, plundered as much treasure as they could, and finally demolished the city. Cortez established his own capital, Mexico City, on the same site.

▶ This picture shows the outline of the Templo Mayor laid over the top of a view of Mexico City as it is today. For many years it was widely believed that the Spanish had built their cathedral on top of the site of the temple when they demolished the Aztec city of Tenochtitlán. But it was discovered buried beneath the city and right next to the Metropolitan Cathedral in 1978.

◀ On top of the Templo Mayor the temple of Tlaloc is on the left, and that of Huitzilopochtli is on the right. The Aztecs' belief system demanded a constant supply of human sacrifices, including the nightly sacrifice to Huitzilopochtli. Often captured in war, the victims would be hacked to death with ritual daggers and their hearts, still beating, would be offered to the god. Special containers collected the blood. The skulls of the dead were then displayed on a "skull rack" at the base of the temple.

Unearthing the great temple

Workers digging tunnels for a subway line in Mexico City in 1978 found something unusual—a stone disk with carvings depicting the dismembered body of a woman. Archaeologists identified it as a representation of Coyolxauhqui, the Aztec Moon goddess. This discovery confirmed that beneath it lay the remains of the Templo Mayor, buried for almost 500 years. At this point the Mexican government stepped in to protect the site, and a systematic excavation began. In five years more than 6,000 precious artifacts were unearthed. Much of the temple was remarkably well preserved, and as archaeologists stripped back the debris of generations, the full splendor of the great temple began to emerge.

The warship *Mary Rose*

On October 11, 1982 more than 60 million people gathered around their TVs to witness an exciting archaeological event. Live pictures were being broadcast of an amazing and historic underwater salvage operation—the raising of part of a 16th-century English warship that had rested on the seabed for more than 400 years since it sank in the summer of 1545. The exciting moment when a long-hidden artifact came to light was shared by an audience worldwide as the *Mary Rose* emerged from the deep.

▲ After the hull section of the long-lost warship had been dug out of the sand and silt, it was placed on a steel cradle and lifted out of the sea by this giant floating crane.

▼ Once it had been raised, the section of the *Mary Rose*'s hull was placed in a specially built dry dock. It is sprayed constantly with cold freshwater to preserve the timbers—if it were allowed to dry out, it would rot away. It has also been coated with a special chemical solution.

Pride of the fleet

The *Mary Rose* was built in Portsmouth, England, on the orders of King Henry VIII (reigned 1509–1547). It was a powerful addition to the Royal Navy and had both the firepower to hole enemy ships at a distance and the maneuverability to get close enough for sailors to board an enemy ship. The surviving timber structure, with its three lines of guns, along with the bronze cannon and other artillery found on the seabed tell us a lot about Tudor ship-building technology and the tactics of naval warfare.

Rediscovery

We know from historical records that the *Mary Rose* sank in the Solent, a stretch of water off of Portsmouth harbor. But its exact location remained a mystery until 1971, when the shattered hull section was discovered on the seabed. Over the next 10 years archaeologists carried out underwater excavations to remove the silt from the wreck and to expose the ship's timbers. Specially trained volunteers carried out thousands of dives. They also retrieved objects that had been used by the ship's crew—including personal possessions such as a whistle, a rosary, and a comb.

▼ This idealized contemporary painting of the *Mary Rose* suggests the pride and admiration it inspired. However, when it sank, it was outdated and worn. It was an easy target for French warships—although some evidence suggests that unseaworthiness was the cause of its sinking.

▲ Underwater archaeology can be very difficult, but it often leads to discoveries of great wealth or importance. This diver has recovered clay jars from the *Glass Wreck*, a ship that sank off the coast of Turkey in the A.D. 1200s with more than 200 pieces of glassware onboard.

Raising the *Mary Rose*

Soon after the wreck had been found engineers decided that it could be brought up to the surface. Underwater archaeologists carried out a series of precise measurements to enable the engineers to build a special steel cradle onto which the hull could be transferred. A huge floating crane was used to lift the wreck off of the seabed and onto the cradle. Then both cradle and hull were lifted out of the sea.

The final clue?

In 2003 archaeologists diving close to where the ship had been discovered found a 16-ft. (5-m) -long piece of wood that they believe is the front section of the ship's keel. If tests show that the age and condition of the wood match those of the hull, then the final piece of the ship will have been found. Archaeologists will have a complete cross section of a Tudor warship.

Battlefield archaeology

▲ French Emperor Napoleon (1769–1821) is pictured leading some of his army. Archaeologists have found evidence along the route of his retreat from Russia back to France that paints a picture of the hardship faced by his soldiers.

Battlefields can be revealing places. Weapons, ammunition, uniforms, and armor unearthed many years after their use paint a vivid picture of the realities of fighting. Eyewitness accounts and other historical records may tell us contradictory stories about a battle. How can we begin to piece together an accurate picture? Often archaeology can help as we turn to the battlefield itself to see what secrets it contains.

Into battle

On the afternoon of June 25, 1876 the banks of the Little Bighorn river in Montana were baked dry by the sweltering sun. By nightfall they had witnessed dramatic and bloody scenes of combat. It was there that General Custer (1839–1876) of the U.S.'s 7th Cavalry led his men into battle for the last time. It was the Battle of Little Bighorn, generally known as "Custer's Last Stand."

A last stand?

This confrontation was part of a series of battles in the 1860s and 1870s between the American army and the armies of Native American peoples, clashing as settlers moved into the natives' traditional homelands. In 1983 an extensive survey of the battlefield at Little Bighorn was carried out after an accidental fire had unexpectedly cleared the ground. More than 2,000 artifacts from the battle were discovered, from cartridge cases and bullets to human remains.

◀ General George Armstrong Custer has been portrayed as a great American hero, but archaeological evidence suggests that his expertise on the battlefield was limited.

The weapons' story

Archaeologists figured out—from the distribution of the shells, analysis of the weapons, and the relative positions of the bodies—where individual weapons had been fired, and where soldiers had moved on the battlefield. They could tell that Custer's men did not face the enemy Sioux warriors in one dramatic last stand, but instead they actually fled from their attackers.

A lost army

Archaeology is constantly telling us more about past battles. In 2002 in Vilnius, Lithuania, builders discovered hundreds of skeletons buried in what appeared to be a mass grave. Examination showed that they dated from the early 1800s. Scraps of uniforms, metal buttons, and army medals dated the grave more precisely. These were the physical remains of part of Napoleon's lost army.

Napoleon Bonaparte, the French emperor, had conquered most of Europe by 1812. That year he planned to conquer Russia. The plan was not a success, and the army had to retreat—just as the winter was setting in. Exhaustion, cold, and starvation killed many of his soldiers. Of the men buried at Vilnius—one of the army's stopping-off points—none appears to have been killed in battle.

Battlefields of World War I

During World War I (1914–1918) millions of soldiers fought and died in the trenches of Europe. For a few people this is still part of their living memory. But for future generations archaeological evidence will be one way of piecing together a picture of life in the trenches. The sites of some of the

▲ Trenches dug during World War I were home to troops, such as these American soldiers in Verdun, France, for months at a time. The battlefields are still full of objects that provide archaeologists with information about how the soldiers spent their time in preparation for battle.

major battles, such as Ypres, Verdun, the Somme, and Passchendaele, still contain the grim evidence of warfare.

Battlefield archaeology can help tell forgotten stories, too. Excavations in the late 1990s found evidence of a World War I trench system in Boesinghe, Belgium. The remains of more than 120 soldiers were also discovered, revealing for the first time the presence of a battlefield that had been overlooked and almost entirely forgotten by history.

▼ The Sioux, Cheyenne, and Arapaho warriors, ferocious and nimble in battle, easily outmaneuvered Custer's men. Armed not only with their traditional weapons but also with the latest and most sophisticated semiautomatic rifles, they succeeded in causing the 7th Cavalry to flee.

City of London

The city of London, England, today is one of the great financial and trading centers of the world. During its long history successive civilizations have thrived there. It has been built and rebuilt many times and is a city of many archaeological layers. Some evidence of London's past can be seen aboveground, but by digging through its underground layers archaeologists have uncovered a wealth of evidence that tells us the fascinating story of the city and its people.

▲▶ The elegant dome of St. Paul's Cathedral (top left), built between 1675 and 1710 after the Great Fire of London, sits in the midst of today's modern office blocks and commercial buildings. Layered beneath the city are many more remains of London's long history.

▼ London is rich in artifacts from Roman times. Archaeologists have unearthed a first-century well made out of barrels, pieces of high-quality glassware, jewelry, crockery, and a writing tablet recording the sale of a slave girl, Fortunata, in c. A.D. 80–120. Objects from later centuries include a hoard of gold coins issued to hospital patients by King Henry VIII (ruled A.D. 1509–1547).

Roman Londinium

The area now covered by London was once countryside, and there is evidence of farming settlements dating back 15,000 years. In the city itself the deepest (and earliest) major layers are Roman, dating from the first century A.D. The Romans were the first to build a bridge across the Thames river, and they built the city to be a trading center of the Roman Empire. Archaeologists have excavated many Roman sites and uncovered the remains of ruined bathhouses, temples, and houses. They have unearthed hundreds of small artifacts, including a find in 2003 of a jar of face cream with the finger marks of its owner still visible!

Medieval London

The Romans left the city in A.D. 410 after their rule collapsed. The area was abandoned for many centuries, but London became an Anglo-Saxon center in the 800s and later fell to the Vikings and then the Normans. By the 1300s the thriving medieval city had become the capital of England. Craftspeople, from goldsmiths and grocers to butchers and bell makers, were powerful, and they have left many traces of their activities. Under Queen Elizabeth I (ruled 1558–1603) London prospered even more, becoming a bustling city of commerce and entertainment. Archaeologists have discovered the remains of the Rose Theatre, where some of William Shakespeare's plays were first performed.

The Great Fire

On September 2, 1666 disaster struck the city. A fire that had started in a baker's shop in a narrow medieval street quickly spread through the adjoining timber houses. Four days later it had destroyed more than 13,000 houses and 87 churches. Excavations in this area often expose a thick deposit of charcoal and baked clay relating to the fire.

The modern city rises

After the Great Fire London was rebuilt once again. A new St. Paul's Cathedral replaced the one that was destroyed in the blaze. The street plans laid out after the fire, with wide roads and spacious squares replacing the cramped medieval streets, became the basis of modern London. Today, in the heart of the city, gleaming skyscrapers tower above the public buildings built in the years since the fire. And as the foundations of a new building are dug, earlier levels of the past come to light—a clay pipe from an 18th-century coffeehouse, a 17th-century helmet from a soldier of the English Civil War, a statue to the Roman god Mithras, or a flint ax head from a time we can hardly imagine.

▼ In 4th-century Londinium wealthy merchants lived in splendid, well-decorated townhouses. The Bucklersbury Pavement, a mosaic tiled floor found near the Bank of England, is a good example. This small area at the heart of London has been the focus of activity for merchants and traders for centuries.

SUMMARY OF CHAPTER 2: TOUCHING THE PAST

The thrill of discovery

People die, but things remain. The houses, cities, and monuments that people build can survive for thousands of years. Sometimes these buildings are remarkably well preserved after hundreds of years, and sometimes they are very run-down or hidden under vegetation or beneath later structures. In this chapter we have uncovered the secrets of some of the most exciting and famous archaeological sites in the world. These places have fascinated generations of archaeologists. Some have been lucky enough to discover famous sites for themselves and to experience the thrill of being the first person to set eyes on something that had been hidden for centuries. Others have looked closer at sites that have already been excavated. All have shared in the excitement of contributing more to our understanding of life in times past.

Aztec feathered shield (c. A.D. 1466–1520) depicting a mythical water creature

More and more clues

As we have seen in this chapter, archaeological sites hold all sorts of clues—big and small—that help archaeologists build up a picture of the people who lived there and the lives they led. The jars found at Tutankhamen's tomb, the preserved food and graffiti in Pompeii, sailors' personal property on the *Mary Rose,* and used ammunition at the battlefield of Little Bighorn—all are just as important in terms of what they tell us as the big, spectacular buildings. Maybe there is a site near you where artifacts have been unearthed that tell a story about the place in times past. If you go to a local museum or join a local archaeology society, you are sure to find out about a lot of exciting information that archaeologists have pieced together. And what about the objects that you use and throw away? One day these objects may be studied by archaeologists in the future. What stories will they tell?

Go further . . .

Play games based on the ancient Egyptians, Greeks, Romans, and Aztecs:
www.gridclub.com/
have_a_go/history/history.shtml

Find a list of World Heritage Sites at:
www.whc.unesco.org/heritage.
htm#debut

Digging up the Past: Pompeii and Herculaneum by Peter Hicks (Hodder Children's Books, 1995)

Valley of the Kings (Digging for the Past) by Smith and Bernard (Oxford University Press, 2003)

Archaeology is Rubbish by Tony Robinson and Mick Aston (Channel 4 Books, 2003)

Architectural historian
Studies the styles and construction of ancient buildings.

Conservationist
Specializes in preserving ancient things, from frescoes and furniture to palaces and temples.

Custodian
Controls galleries and archaeological sites to protect them from damage and theft and looks after displays so that members of the public can visit.

Filmmaker or documentary maker
Uses history and archaeology as a starting point for their imaginations in recreating past worlds for movies or TV.

Visit the Museum of London for a trip through time, exploring London from its prehistoric origins to the present day:
London, England EC2Y 5HN
Phone: 44 0870 444 3851
www.museumoflondon.org.uk

See the *Mary Rose*:
Portsmouth Historic Dockyard
Portsmouth, England
Phone: 44 023 9281 2931
www.maryrose.org

Explore the Acropolis at the Acropolis Museum
Athens, Greece
www.culture.gr/2/21/211/21101m/
e211am01.html

Glossary

A.D.
Anno Domini—a religious dating system in which 1 B.C. is equivalent to A.D. 1.

aerial photography
A method of studying a site using photographs taken from the air.

afterlife
Eternal or everlasting life after death. Most religions and cultures believe in some form of afterlife.

alignment
A row of objects positioned so that they are in line with something else, such as the rising Sun or the Moon and stars, at certain times of the year.

amphitheater
A semicircular space used for public performances and surrounded by tiers of seats, invented by the ancient Greeks.

amulet
A type of ornament worn as a charm against evil spirits.

Anglo-Saxon
Belonging to a period of English history from the end of the Roman Empire (A.D. 476) to the Norman Conquest (A.D. 1066).

aqueduct
A bridgelike structure built to channel water from place to place.

archaeology
The study of the past using careful analysis and scientific examination of material remains, carried out by archaeologists.

artifact
An object made by humans.

artillery
Heavy weapons. Also the part of an army that uses artillery in battle.

Aztecs People of the Aztec civilization dominant in Mexico from the A.D. 1100s to the 1500s.

B.C.
Before Christ—a religious dating system in which 1 B.C. is equivalent to A.D. 1.

Bronze Age
The second stage in a three-stage classification of prehistoric time when people started using bronze to make weapons and tools. In Europe this happened between c. 3000 B.C. and 800 B.C.

burial mound
A mound of dirt or stones containing bodies of the dead.

carbon dating
A scientific method of dating an organic object such as wood, other plant remains, or human remains.

cave art
Pictures painted or etched onto the walls of caves by prehistoric people.

celestial
Relating to the sky or the heavens.

citadel
A defensive fortification built high up off the ground to protect a town or city against attacks.

civilization
A highly advanced culture or society.

commerce
Buying and selling.

conquistador
One of the Spanish soldier-adventurers who conquered much of South and Central America in the A.D. 1500s.

crusader
A participant in one of the military expeditions led by European Christians to seize Jerusalem from the Muslims between the A.D. 1000s and 1200s.

currency
Something used as a medium of exchange when buying and selling—usually, though not always, money.

dig
An archaeological excavation.

DNA
A chemical found inside all living things. It carries information that is unique to each individual but is similar in individuals who are related to each other. Scientists can examine the DNA in ancient human remains and find out if bodies found close to each other were related.

empire
A collection of countries ruled by another country and its leaders.

excavation
The process of digging up a site in order to find archaeological evidence.

fertility
When referring to land, plants, or crops, the ability to produce abundant harvests.

flint
A hard stone used for making early prehistoric tools and weapons.

fortifications
Defensive structures, such as walls and moats, built to protect a settlement against attacks.

fortress
A heavily fortified structure.

foundations
The supporting level of stone, brick, or concrete on top of which structures are built. Often the remains of foundations last after buildings have fallen down or been destroyed.

fragment
A small part detached from a larger object.

fresco
A wall painting.

frieze
A decorative strip painted or sculpted along the top edge of a wall.

geophysics
The study of Earth's physical properties. Geophysics can help archaeologists figure out where there are structures lying underground.

hallucinogenic
Causing unusual dreams or visions.

hieroglyphs
Picture writing invented by the ancient Egyptians.

hull
The main body of a ship.

hunter-gatherer
A member of a small nomadic community who lives by hunting, fishing, and collecting wild food such as honey, nuts, and berries.

Incas
The people of the central Andes region of South America whose empire was at its peak in the A.D. 1500s

Iron Age
The third prehistoric period of classification when iron was used to make tools and weapons. In Europe this was from c. 800 B.C. until the beginning of the Roman period (c. 100 B.C.).

keel
The timber or metal base of a ship—the part that is below the waterline.

legend
A traditional story that does not necessarily have a firm basis in historical fact.

Mayan
Relating to the civilization and people of southern Mexico between c. A.D. 300 and A.D. 900.

medieval
Relating to the Middle Ages of European history, from around the A.D. 400s to the A.D 1400s.

megalith
A large prehistoric stone monument found in northern Europe.

metropolis
A very large city.

Moors
The Arab Muslims of North Africa who colonized Spain between the A.D. 700s and A.D. 1400s.

mosque
A place of worship for Muslim people.

mummy
A preserved human body. It may have been preserved deliberately, such as in the case of ancient Egyptian mummies, or it may have been preserved naturally under certain conditions.

myth
A legend or traditional story often involving gods and goddesses or other supernatural beings and usually culturally very important to the society to which it belongs.

Native American
Relating to the earliest inhabitants of North and South America and their descendants, rather than settlers who arrived from Europe from the A.D. 1400s onward.

nomad
A member of a community who moves from place to place without settling permanently.

Norman Conquest
The conquest of England by the Normans, led by King William I in A.D. 1066.

Paleolithic
Relating to the early Stone Age, a vast period of time stretching from around 2.5 million years ago, when the first artifacts were made, to around 13,000 B.C.

passage grave
A tomb reached by moving along a horizontal passage. Passage graves were commonly built in northern Europe around 3000 B.C.

pharaoh
An ancient Egyptian ruler.

plaza
A square or formal space in a town or city.

prehistory
The time before written records existed. This period varies around the world because writing was developed at different times by different cultures.

Pueblo
Relating to the Native American peoples of New Mexico and Arizona and to their culture.

pyramid
A monument that is square at the base and pointed at the top. The most famous pyramids are the ancient Egyptian tombs.

radar
A method of finding objects by sending out radio waves and analyzing their echoes.

radioactivity
Energy generated by the disintegration of atoms (tiny particles from which all substances are made) over time.

ramparts
High defensive boundaries running around the edge of a fortified building, town, or city.

replica
A copy of something.

ritual
A formal (often religious) action performed in a solemn way.

rosary
A string of beads used to aid devotion during prayer.

sacrifice
The killing of an animal or person as an offering to a higher power or god.

satellite imaging
The use of satellite technology to provide overhead views of archaeological sites. Satellite images often show patterns of structures under the ground.

settlement
A place where a group of people live together for a long period of time. Farms, villages, towns, cities, and palaces are all settlements.

shrine
A special place set aside to honor a person or a god.

Stone Age
The first (and earliest) of the three classifications of prehistory when stone was used for tools and weapons. It is a long period of time dating back to the earliest origins of humankind. In Europe it ended after 3000 B.C. when the Bronze Age began.

strata (singular: stratum)
Layers of material left behind by people or things at successive times in history and prehistory. The study of these various levels of material helps archaeologists date the objects they find.

Sumerian
Relating to the ancient Mesopotamian civilization of Sumer, which began to develop around 3000 B.C., and to its people. Ur was one of the Sumerian city-states.

temple
A building constructed for religious worship.

terra-cotta
Baked clay often used to make ornaments, pottery, and statues.

trench
A long, narrow ditch. Archaeologists often dig trenches as part of their excavation of a site. Trenches were also a feature of battlefields in World War I, where they served as a place of shelter for soldiers and a location for the fighting itself.

urban
Relating to a town or city.

Viking
One of the Scandinavian warrior groups who invaded Europe between the A.D. 700s and A.D. 1000s.

X-ray
A type of radiation used to reveal things hidden beneath something else such as bones in a person's body or a mummy inside a stone coffin.

ziggurat
A step-sided pyramid prominent in the cityscapes of ancient Mesopotamia.

Index

Acknowledgments

The publisher would like to thank the following for permission to reproduce their material. Every care has been taken to trace copyright holders. However, if there have been unintentional omissions or failure to trace copyright holders, we apologize and will, if informed, endeavor to make corrections in any future edition.

Key: *b* = bottom, *c* = center, *l* = left, *r* = right, *t* = top

Cover *l* Art Archive; Cover *c* Art Archive; Cover *r* Art Archive; Cover *background* Getty; 1 Corbis; 2–3 Corbis 4–5 Corbis; 7 Getty; 8*tl* Pitt Rivers Museum, Oxford; 8*cr* Corbis; 9*t* AKG, London; 10–11 Corbis; 12*tl* Science Photo Library (SPL); 12*bl* Art Archive; 12–13 Skyscan; 13*br* Art Archive; 14*cr* Art Archive; 14*bl* Corbis; 14–15 Art Archive; 15*t* Corbis; 15*b* Art Archive; 16*tl* Art Archive; 17*t* British Museum; 18*tl* Corbis; 18*bl* National Geographic Image Collection; 19*tc* Getty News; 19*bc* Rex Features; 19*r* Corbis; 20–21*t* Corbis; 20*bl* SPL; 21*tc* Corbis; 21*bl* David Ford; 22*cl* British Museum; 23*t* British Museum; 24*tl* Art Archive; 24*bl* Corbis; 25*tr* Corbis; 25*b* Corbis; 26*tl* Art Archive; 26*cr* Art Archive; 28*tl* Art Archive; 28*bl* Corbis; 28–29 Art Archive; 29*t* Michael Fox; 29*b* Alamy; 30–31 Corbis; 31*c* Hulton Getty; 31*tcl* Art Archive; 32*tl* British Museum; 32*bl* British Museum; 34*tl* Bridgeman Art Library; 34*cr* British Museum; 34*bl* Corbis; 35 Corbis; 36–37 Art Archive; 36*br* Corbis; 37*tr* Corbis; 37*br* Getty; 38*tl* Alamy; 38–39 Art Archive; 39*b* Art Archive; 40*tl* Art Archive; 40*cr* NGIC; 40*b* Corbis; 41*tr* Corbis; 41*b* Corbis; 42*tl* AKG, London; 42*b* AKG, London; 43*l* Corbis; 43*tr* Corbis; 43*br* Corbis; 44*l* Corbis; 44–45 Corbis; 45*tr* Corbis; 46*tr* Werner Foreman Archive; 47*tr* Corbis; 48*tr* Werner Foreman Archive; 48*b* Art Archive; 49*l* Art Archive; 49*tr* Corbis; 50*tl* Scala; 50*cr* Art Archive; 51*tr* David Hiser/Aspen Photographers; 52*tl* The Mary Rose Trust; 52*bl* The Mary Rose Trust; 52–53 Art Archive; 53*tr* Corbis; 54*tl* Art Archive; 54*bl* Corbis; 54–55 Corbis; 55*tr* Corbis; 55*cl* Corbis; 55*br* Corbis; 58*cl* Art Archive; 59*br* Corbis; 60*b* Corbis; 62–63 Corbis; 64 Corbis

The publisher would like to thank the following illustrators:
Roger Hutchins 31; Steve Weston (Linden Artists) 8–9, 11, 16–17, 26–27, 32–33, 36, 46–47, 50–51, 56–57.

The author would like to thank Catherine for the care and hard work she put into editing the text and Pete for the design. Not forgetting Gill, who commissioned the book in the first place.